THE BATTLE OF CAMPBELL'S STATION

16 NOVEMBER 1863

# THE BATTLE OF CAMPBELL'S STATION

## 16 NOVEMBER 1863

### GERALD L. AUGUSTUS

Cherohala Press
Cleveland, Tennessee

The Battle of Campbell's Station
16 November 1863

Published by Cherohala Press, an imprint of CPT Press
900 Walker ST NE
Cleveland, TN 37311
USA
email: cptpress@pentecostaltheology.org
website: www.cptpress.com

Library of Congress Control Number: 2013948946

ISBN-10: 1935931369
ISBN-13: 9781935931362

# CONTENTS

**Chapter 10**

## List of Maps and Illustrations

# Preface

This book is my interpretation of what happened in the fall of 1863 at Campbell's Station and may differ from previous versions. Based on the accounts left by the participants in this battle along with later accounts, I have come to the conclusion that the following narrative explains what happened.

Looking at the text and footnotes, the reader will see a predominance of Northern accounts and far fewer Southern accounts. The reason for this is no prejudice on the part of the author, but only reflects the amount of writings by the participants in the battle. Primary sources have been used as much as possible.

The military conflict which occurred between 1861 and 1865 has had as many as thirty some odd names including the most popular name today 'Civil War'. It has been and in some cases is still referred to as the War Between the States, War of the Rebellion, War of Northern Aggression, War Between the North and South, The War of 1861, The Confederate War, The Lost Cause, The War of the Sixties, The Late Unpleasantness, etc. To my grandparents, whose parents had survived that time period, it was simply 'The War'. All other wars in history had names, but the 1861-1865 era was simply 'The War'. Many people will take offence at the use of many of the names for the conflict in which over 620,000 lives were lost; therefore, I have used the term 'The War' in this book.[1]

The Confederate reports of the Battle of Campbell's Station refer to Hood's Division. General John B. Hood in November 1863 was recuperating from the amputation of his right leg from injuries received in the Battle of Chickamauga in September of that year. In November 1863 the division was lead by General Micah Jenkins, and the division will always be referred to in this work as Jenkins' Division. General Jenkins' former brigade will be referred to as

---

[1] Burke Davis, *The Civil War: Strange & Fascinating Facts* (New York: Wings Books, 1982), pp. 79-80.

Bratton's Brigade for Colonel John Bratton who led the brigade in the late fall of 1863.

In this book the troops of the United States will be referred to as Federals, Northerners, United States or U.S. troops. The soldiers of the Confederate States will be referred to as Confederates or Southerners.

Until 1889, the Tennessee River began where the Holston River met the Little Tennessee River at present day Lenoir City. When the United States government made plans to dredge the channels of the primary rivers, but not the tributaries in the eastern United States, the people in Knoxville became very concerned that an improved channel would not reach them. An act of the Tennessee Legislature in 1889 declared that the Tennessee River began at Kingsport, Tennessee. The next year the United States Congress changed the beginning of the Tennessee River to its present location above Knoxville where the Holston and French Broad Rivers join together. By this change, Knoxville could have a cleared channel all the way to their city at the expense of the United States government.[2]

During the 1860's, there was no Standard Time as there is today. Time zones and a standard time within the zone did not come about until years after the War. Until then, each community had their own time, and even people within the community might have different times. The time pieces that existed often ran too slow or too fast so that many people had many different times of day at the same time. Reports as to what time something happened, even among officers in the same division, corps, or army, varied sometimes as much as an hour apart. Interestingly, in modern Eastern Standard Time, the sunrise on 16 November 1863 occurred at 7.14 am and sunset was at 5.27 pm.[3]

---

[2] Carroll Van West, *The Tennessee Encyclopedia of History and Culture* (Nashville, TN: The Tennessee Historical Society, 1998), p. 944.

[3] www.timeanddate.com

# Acknowledgements

Writing a book is in some ways a lonely experience, but at the same time no book of historical nature can be successfully completed without the help and/or encouragement of others. These are a few of the people who have materially aided in this book.

Christopher L. Augustus, my son, has always helped his father with the computer, and produced the wonderful accompanying maps.

Sandra M. Augustus, my wife and best friend, has always encouraged me in writing. Even though she had promised never to read another manuscript for corrections after my last book, she again helped with this one.

Julia J. Barham, Farragut Folklife Museum Coordinator, has tirelessly encouraged and helped me.

Bob Linsel, formerly of the Farragut Folklife Museum, did everything he could to encourage me to write this book. Everyone down here in Tennessee misses him since he moved to be closer to his grandchildren.

Jerry Keyes, whose work both in research and field work have made him an expert on the Battle of Campbell's Station, unselfishly shared his vast knowledge with me which has made this a better interpretation.

Louis La Marche, Farragut Folklife Museum, pushed me to construct an Order of Battle for the Battle of Campbell's Station and made so many good suggestions to improve the narrative.

Stephen T. Moriak, my son in law, who has been such an aid to me in helping with the intricacies of the computer.

Joe Spence, educator, historian, and friend, agreed to read and suggest improvements in this book. As always, his editing improved the readability of the text.

John Christopher Thomas, editor/publisher and one of my former students, and his colleague Lee Roy Martin, whose diligent work, questioning, and suggestions have made this a much better book.

# 1

## THE UNION OCCUPATION

The Tennessee Valley was of great importance to both sides in the War. Besides vast supplies of corn, wheat, hogs, horses, and mules, there were the two railroads. The East Tennessee and Georgia Railroad ran from Knoxville to Cleveland, Tennessee, where the track spilt with one track preceding to Chattanooga and the other to Dalton, Georgia. The East Tennessee and Virginia Railroad ran from Knoxville to Bristol, Virginia. They were of major importance to the Confederacy because this was a direct route for troops and supplies to move from the Western Confederacy to Virginia and visa versa.[1]

The major supply of salt and lead for the Confederacy was in Southwestern Virginia, and the major supply of copper was in Southeastern Tennessee. In addition to denying the Confederates all of the above, East Tennessee was very important to the Federal government because East Tennesseans were overwhelmingly Unionist in sentiment, and they suffered under Confederate occupation.

East Tennessee had been under Confederate control from 1861 to the fall of 1863 when the situation changed. Union Major General Ambrose Burnside moved into East Tennessee from Kentucky in September 1863 with the 23rd Corps of the Army of the Ohio.

---

[1] James Burns, 'The Hiwassee East Tennessee and Georgia Railroad (Athens, Tennessee', *The Daily Post-Athenian, Sesqui-Centennial Edition*, 10 June 1969, p. 14A; W. Todd Groce, *Mountain Rebels: East Tennessee Confederates and the Civil War, 1860-1870* (Knoxville, TN: The University of Tennessee, 1999), pp. 9-13.

He was soon joined by the first two Divisions of the 9th Corps from the Army of the Potomac, coming from Vicksburg, Mississippi, which had fallen on 4 July 1863. After Knoxville was captured, the Federal troops moved up and down the valley to occupy the central portion of the Great Valley of East Tennessee. They had gone as far south as the Hiwasee River and made contact with Chattanooga. At the same time that Burnside captured the Knoxville area, Union Major General William Rosecrans had maneuvered Confederate General Braxton Bragg out of Middle Tennessee and then flanked Bragg out of Chattanooga. On 19 and 20 September 1863, during the Battle of Chickamauga, Confederate General Bragg's army was reinforced with two divisions of Confederate General James Longstreet's 1st Corps of the Army of Northern Virginia. The battle was a major defeat for the Union army and resulted in Union General Rosecrans falling back into Chattanooga, where Confederate General Bragg's army lay siege to the city. Rosecrans would soon be relieved from command, and Major General Ulysses S. Grant would become the commander in Chattanooga.[2]

General James Longstreet, as well as many of the generals serving under Bragg, could not agree with decisions Bragg made after the Battle of Chickamauga. In fact, Longstreet was one of the major leaders in a movement by many of the generals to have Bragg replaced as the commander. Confederate President Jefferson Davis visited the army and met with the generals, but continued to support Bragg and retain him in command.

Then Bragg, against his generals urging, and with the agreement of Confederate President Jefferson Davis, detached Longstreet and his Corps to move up the valley to retake Knoxville and reopen the supply routes from Virginia. A Confederate force under command of General Carter Stevenson had begun moving toward Knoxville in late October but was recalled when Bragg sent Longstreet instead. Longstreet's Corps began to move by railroad toward Knoxville in November 1863.

---

[2] Ezar J. Warner, *Generals in Blue: Lives of the Union Commanders* (Baton Rouge, LA: Louisiana State University Press, 1988), pp. 185, 411; William C. Davis (ed.), *The Confederate General*, IV (Harrisburg, PA: National Historical Society, 1991), p. 92.

## Ambrose Everett Burnside
## Union Commander

Figure 1
**Major General Ambrose E. Burnside**
**Commander of the Army of the Ohio**
(From the Farragut Folklife Museum Collections)

Ambrose E. Burnside (1824-1888) was born in Indiana and graduated from West Point in 1847. He resigned his commission in 1853 and moved to Bristol, Rhode Island and formed a company to manufacture the breech loading rifle that he had designed. The venture failed, and Burnside sold his interest in the company to others who reorganized and continued to manufacture Burnside's invention. Prior to and during the War, the United States purchased over 53,000 Burnside Carbines.

In 1861 Burnside organized and became colonel of the 1st Rhode Island Infantry and was in command of a brigade at First Manassas in July 1861. He was commissioned a brigadier general as of 6 August 1861. For his 'eminently successful' expedition to invade the coast of North Carolina, he was promoted to major general as of 18 March 1862. At the Battle of Sharpsburg in September 1862, Burnside made a serious tactical mistake of ordering his men to cross a narrow bridge over Antietam Creek. The bridge was defended by a relatively small number of Confederates who could concentrate their fire on the bridge. The creek could have been easily waded, and the Union forces could have attacked the rest of the Confederates and probably won the battle.

Burnside reluctantly accepted the command of the Army of the Potomac on 10 November 1862. At the Battle of Fredericksburg, Virginia, his unsuccessful attacks resulted in over 13,000 casualties. After Fredericksburg, he tried to flank the Confederates, which resulted in the disastrous 'Mud March'. Burnside was then relieved from command of the Army of the Potomac and returned to command of the 9th Corps.

In March 1863 Burnside was assigned to command the Department of the Ohio and the Army of the Ohio. With the 23rd Corps of his new command, he successfully captured Knoxville and the surrounding area of East Tennessee. After his masterful retreat to Knoxville and the lifting of the siege of that city, Burnside, at his own request, was relieved from command due to health problems.

By the time the 9th Corps was returned to Virginia in the spring of 1864, Burnside had recovered his health enough to resume command of the 9th Corps. He became involved in controversy again due to his planning of the Battle of the Crater, and he eventually resigned on 15 April 1865. After the War Burnside was elected three times as governor of Rhode Island and was serving in the United States Senate when he died.[3]

---

[3] Warner, *Generals in Blue*, pp. 57-58.

## James Longstreet
## Confederate Commander

Figure 2
**Lieutenant General James Longstreet**
**Commander of the Confederate Troops**
(From the Farragut Folklife Museum Collections)

James Longstreet (1821-1904) was born in South Carolina and grew up in Georgia and Alabama. He graduated from West Point in 1842 and was wounded in 1847 during the Mexican War. Longstreet married Maria L. Garland whose cousin, Julia Dent, was the wife of Ulysses S. Grant. He was a major in the U.S. Army when he resigned in June 1861 to join the Confederate Army as a brigadier general. Longstreet was promoted to major general in October 1861 and lieutenant general in October 1862.

Longstreet's performance in many battles earned him the praise of Robert E. Lee who referred to Longstreet as 'my old war horse.' His differences with General Lee and lack of aggressiveness during the Battle of Gettysburg in July 1863 changed many people's opinion of Longstreet during the War and especially after the War.

In September 1863, Longstreet and two divisions of his corps had been sent to northern Georgia to reinforce the Army of Tennessee. Longstreet's attack on 20 September 1863 in the Battle of Chickamauga happened to occur just as a gap appeared in the Union line. The Confederates moved through the gap and created a major victory for the south.

Longstreet and many of the generals in the Army of Tennessee felt that Chickamauga was a hollow victory. They felt that commander Braxton Bragg should have attacked Chattanooga as the Union army retreated instead of creating a siege. The bickering among the Southern generals reached such proportions that Confederate President Jefferson Davis came to try to settle the argument. Davis felt he had settled the problem, but he had not.

In November of 1863, Longstreet's two divisions were ordered to recapture Knoxville. This led to the Battle of Campbell's Station, the siege of Knoxville, and the attack on Fort Sanders in November 1863. Longstreet next learned that Union General William T. Sherman with a large force of men had been sent to reinforce the Union troops in Knoxville and that the Confederates had been defeated at Chattanooga.

Unable to rejoin the Army of Tennessee, Longstreet's forces moved to the northeastern part of Tennessee. Staying there until spring 1864, they returned to the Army of Northern Virginia. During the Battle of the Wilderness in May 1864, Longstreet was seriously injured, and Micah Jenkins was killed by friendly fire. Longstreet was not able to resume command until late fall and was with General Lee at the Appomattox surrender.

In the post war years, Longstreet became a close friend of Ulysses S. Grant who appointed him U.S. Minister to Turkey. He also became a Republican, and he questioned some of Robert E. Lee's decisions. To the large majority of former Confederates, such actions were intolerable. Therefore to many southerners, Longstreet was blamed for the loss of the Battle of Gettysburg and thus the entire War.[4]

---

[4] Ezar J. Warner, *Generals in Gray: Lives of the Confederate Commanders* (Baton Rouge, LA: Louisiana State University Press, 1988), pp. 192-93; David, *The Confederate General*, pp. 91-95.

## Excursus 1

### The Feuding Confederate Generals

Evander McIvor Law versus Micah Jenkins and James Longstreet

Brigadier General Evander McIvor Law (1836-1920) and Brigadier General Micah Jenkins (1835-1864) were both graduates of the South Carolina Military Academy (The Citadel), the former in 1856 and the latter in 1854. According to rumor, they were rivals in school even though Jenkins was two years ahead. Both became teachers at Kings Mountain Military Academy in South Carolina. Law moved in 1860 to co-found the Military High School in Tuskegee, Alabama.

Both men left their schools in 1861 with Jenkins as colonel of the 5th South Carolina Infantry and Law as lieutenant colonel of the 4th Alabama Infantry. Law became the colonel of the regiment at the death of the colonel. Jenkins was promoted to brigadier general to date from 22 July 1862. Law was promoted to brigadier general on 2 October 1862.

Law's Alabama Brigade was in General James Longstreet's Corps during the Gettysburg Campaign in 1863. He was the senior brigade commander when Law's division commander General John B. Hood was severely wounded on 2 July 1863. Law took command of the division for the rest of the Gettysburg Battle, retreat, and for about two and half months until the return of General Hood. Jenkins' Brigade had been left in Virginia during this campaign.

When Longstreet's Corps was sent to Georgia to reinforce General Braxton Bragg's Army of Tennessee, Law's Brigade was in the Battle of Chickamauga; while Jenkins' Brigade arrived afterwards due to poor condition of the railroads. During the Battle of Chickamauga, Hood was again severely wounded, and again Law took charge of the division. When the amputation of Hood's leg lead to a long recuperation, Longstreet appointed Jenkins to command the division.

Longstreet was not satisfied with Law's performance on several occasions. At Suffolk, Virginia, Law had two companies of men captured; and at Gettysburg, Law had questioned Longstreet's orders to the point that Longstreet considered him to have 'bordered on insubordination'. Longstreet further felt that late arrival of Law's Brigade led to the repulse of Longstreet's attack on Little Round Top at Gettysburg. At the Battle of Wauhatchie, Tennessee, just south of Chattanooga on 28 October 1863, Jenkins blamed Law for their failure to defeat the Federals. Longstreet had considered relieving Law from command but did not.

The regimental commanders in the division signed a petition for Law to be retained as division commander. Jenkins realized that his taking command of the division would cause problems but thought that he could overcome any resentment. Longstreet dismissed the petition and placed Jenkins in command. Longstreet's official reason was that Jenkins' commission as brigadier general was months earlier then Laws. The usual military custom was that the earliest commissioned officer automatically assumed the leadership position in the absence of the commander.

At Campbell's Station, Jenkins and Longstreet criticized Law for failing to get around the left flank of Burnside's army. Years later, the animosity was still so strong that Longstreet even repeated the unfounded rumor that 'Law said he might have made the attack successfully, but that Jenkins would have reaped the credit of it, and hence he delayed until the enemy got out of the way.'

The conflict between Law and Longstreet continued after Campbell's Station, and Law tried to resign and be transferred to the cavalry. Longstreet brought charges of misconduct against Law. He even threatened to resign if Law was not court-martialed. Not wanting to lose the valuable services of either man, the Confederate War Department ignored the whole matter and left both men in their positions.

Law returned with Longstreet's Corps to Virginia and was severely wounded at Cold Harbor on 2 June 1864. After recovering from that wound, he was sent to South Carolina to lead a cavalry brigade. Law evidently got along well with his new commanders and was recommended and received his commission as major general on 20 March 1865. After the War, Law became a farmer, was associated with the King's Mountain Military Academy, and established the South Florida Military and Educational Institute.[5]

Robertson versus Longstreet

Jerome Bonaparte Robertson (1815-1891) was born in Kentucky, attended Transylvania University in Kentucky, and earned a medical degree in 1835. In 1836, Robertson went to Texas to help the Texans gain independence from Mexico. Returning home briefly, he returned to Texas to farm and practice medicine.

When the War came in 1861, Robertson raised and was captain of Company I, 5th Texas Infantry. By October 1861, he was appointed lieutenant colonel and when the Colonel James J. Archer was promoted to general, Robertson became the regiment's colonel. When Robertson's brigade commander John B. Hood was promoted major general, Robertson was promoted to brigadier general in November 1862.

After the Battle of Wauhatchie, Tennessee, Longstreet was very irritated at not destroying the Union forces. He blamed generals Evander Law and Robertson for the failure. Longstreet considered the suspension of both generals but decided to relieve only Robertson from command on 1 November 1863. General Braxton Bragg, the Confederate commander at Chattanooga, reviewed the case against Robertson and restored him to command.

Bragg gave the reason that Longstreet needed Robertson in his attempt to capture Knoxville. However, there may have been more sinister reasons. Longstreet had been a leader in the group of generals who attempted to have Bragg removed from his command. Too, Bragg owed the Robertson family a debt. After the Battle of Murfreesboro, Bragg tried to blame General John C. Breckinridge for the Confederate defeat. Robertson's son, Felix H. Robertson, was an artillery commander who 'perjured' himself in an attempt to blame Breckinridge.

In December 1863 after Campbell's Station and Knoxville, Robertson was charged with 'insulting the generalship and judgment of Brigadier General Micah Jenkins his immediate superior'. Robertson was found guilty of misconduct and suspended. Robertson re-

---

[5] Davis, *The Confederate General*, Volume I, pp. 162-67; Volume IV, pp. 23-24; Medoza, *Confederate Struggle For Command*, pp. 85-88; Longstreet, *From Manassas to Appomattox*, p. 495.

turned to Texas and commanded the state reserves. After the War he became a successful businessman.[6]

Lafayette McLaws versus James Longstreet

Lafayette McLaws (1821-1897) was from Georgia and graduated from West Point in 1842 with James Longstreet. He fought in the War with Mexico and was a captain in the U. S. Army in 1861 when he resigned and was appointed a major in the Confederate Army. McLaws quickly rose to the rank of brigadier general by 25 September 1861 and major general on 23 May 1862 in command of a division.

During the Battle of Chancellorsville in May 1863, General Robert E. Lee was very critical of McLaws for not moving his troops fast enough. McLaws was passed over for promotion to command 'Stonewall' Jackson's Corps after Jackson's death. James Longstreet, McLaws' good friend, claimed that he had not received the Corps command, because he was not a Virginian.

The McLaws and Longstreet friendship came to a bitter end during the Gettysburg Campaign in July 1863. McLaws thought that Longstreet was 'a humbug, a man of small capacity, very obstinate, not at all chivalrous, exceedingly conceited, and totally selfish'. When Longstreet and other generals attempted to remove Braxton Bragg from command of the Army of Tennessee after Chickamauga, McLaws refused to take Longstreet's side. After the disastrous Confederate attack on Fort Sanders in Knoxville, Longstreet brought charges against McLaws. In the court-martial, McLaws was found innocent of all charges, except for 'failing in details of his attack to make arrangements essential to success'. On this charge, McLaws was found guilty and sentenced to a sixty day suspension without pay. The sentence was overturned by the Richmond authorities, and McLaws was returned to duty.

McLaws, however, did not return to his old command. He was assigned to the defenses of Savannah. McLaws was financially ruined by the War. Even his old friend U.S. Grant tried to find gov-

---

[6] Davis, *The Confederate General*, Volume III, pp. 162-67; Volume IV, pp. 23-24; Mendoza, *Confederate Struggle For Command*, p. 110.

ernment employment for him, but he lived out his life in an impoverished state.[7]

---

[7] Davis, *The Confederate General*, Volume IV, pp. 121-31; McLaws, *A Soldier's General*, pp. 43-46.

# 2

## LONGSTREET ADVANCES

Concerned that that the Confederates would send a large army from Chattanooga to recapture Knoxville, Union General Burnside decided to move all of his troops from south of the Tennessee River to the north side at Loudon, Tennessee. The $2^{nd}$ Division of the $23^{rd}$ Corps was camped opposite Loudon, and most of the two Divisions of the $9^{th}$ Corps were located at Lenoirs Station (present day Lenoir City).[1] [See Appendix A, for The Order of Battle.]

In November 1863, Major General Ulysses S. Grant with his headquarters in Chattanooga was in command of all Federal troops in Tennessee. Grant sent Colonel James H. Wilson and Assistant Secretary of War Charles A. Dana with orders for General Burnside to draw Confederate General James Longstreet's forces to Knoxville and hold them there until the Confederates at Chattanooga could be defeated. Burnside was reluctant to follow these orders due to lack of supplies. Burnside had planned to cross over to the eastern side of the Holston River, which had not been as heavily raided for food as the Knoxville side of the river. Wilson and Dana were finally able to convince Burnside to follow orders at the very time as the Confederates were crossing the Tennessee River.[2] [See Map 1. Longstreet Advances.]

---

[1] United States War Department: *The War of the Rebellion: A Compilation of the Official Records of the Union and Confederate Armies* 128 Volumes, Volume 31, Part 1 (Harrisburg, PA: The National Historical Society, 1971 reprint of 1880-1901 edition), p. 811.

[2] James H. Wilson, *Under the Old Flag: Recollections of Military Operations in the War for the Union, The Spanish War, The Boxer Rebellion, Etc.* (Lexington, KY: Forgotten Books, 2012), pp. 281-86.

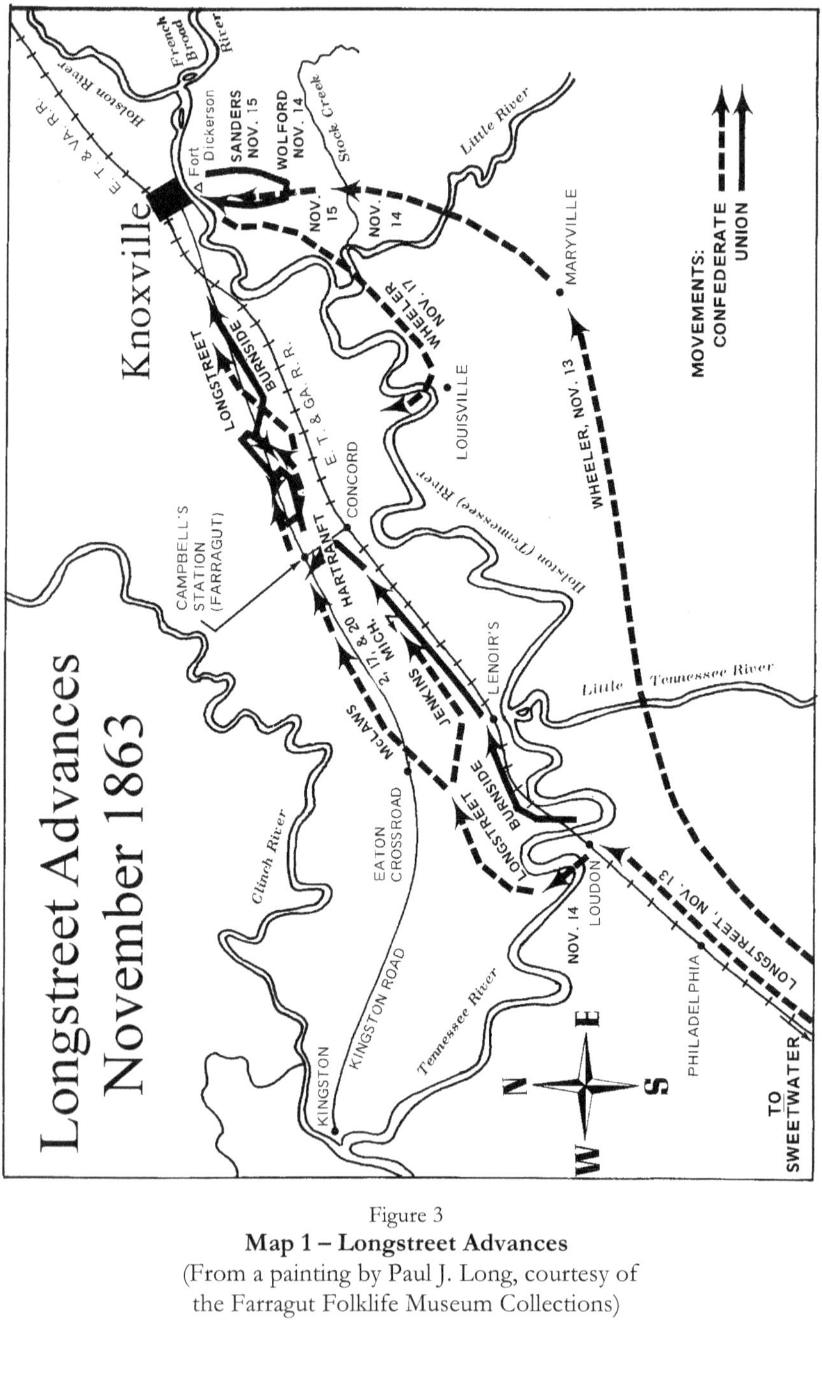

Figure 3
**Map 1 – Longstreet Advances**
(From a painting by Paul J. Long, courtesy of
the Farragut Folklife Museum Collections)

Confederate General James Longstreet would have preferred to have bypassed the Union troops at Loudon and moved to the east across the Little Tennessee River and then to Knoxville. The lack of animals and wagons to move his pontoon boats forced Longstreet to cross the Tennessee River near and down river from Loudon at Huff's Ferry. The four gun Battery E of Major Austin Leyden's 9th Georgia Artillery had to be left at Loudon for lack of animals to pull it to Campbell's Station and beyond. Huff's Ferry was less than a mile from the railroad at Loudon, but because of a bend in the Tennessee River, it was about six miles from where the 23rd Corps troops were camped.[3] [See Map 1.]

The Confederates who crossed the Tennessee River at Huff's Ferry lacked shoes and warm clothing. One of the soldiers described Longstreet's army: 'A great number of our men were barefooted, some with shoes partly worn out, clothes ragged and torn, not an overcoat or extra garment among the line officers or men throughout the army, as all surplus baggage had been left in Virginia. But when the battle was about to show up the soldiers were on hand, ready and willing as of old, to plunge headlong into the fray.' Even some of the infantry officers were shoeless.[4] [See Appendix A for the Order of Battle.]

Even though the Confederates had major clothing problems, they were well supplied with rifle muskets, ammunition, and accoutrements. The only ordnance problem was the poor fuses for their artillery projectiles. Some of the ammunition and ordnance stores had just arrived, as they prepared to board the trains for the trip to Loudon. Longstreet's Corps was also deficient in horse harnesses and wagons to carry the ammunition and other supplies.[5]

During the night of November 13 and 14, 1863, the Confederates began to place a pontoon bridge across the Tennessee River. Union General Burnside was still somewhat undecided as to his

---

[3] Wilson, *Under the Old Flag*, pp. 456-57, 478.

[4] D. Augustus Dickert, *History of Kershaw's Brigade* (Wilmington, NC: Broadfoot Publishing Company, 1990 reprint of the 1899 edition), p. 302; Richard Lewis, *Camp Life of a Confederate Boy, Bratton's Brigade, Longstreet's Corps, C.S.A.* (Gaithersburg, MD: Butternut Press, 1984), p. 70.

[5] Janet B. Hewett (ed.), *Supplement to the Official Records of the Union and Confederate Armies*, 100 Volumes (Serial 5; Wilmington, NC: Broadfoot Publishing Company, 1994-2001), pp. 684-85.

next move. He sent troops to stop the Confederates and then withdrew them before contact was made. Next, he decided to drive them back into the Tennessee River. Marching back and forth churned up the muddy roads even more. As the Federal troops tried to return to Huff's Ferry, they met the vanguard of the Confederates near a church (modern day New Providence Baptist where the huge cross is located on Interstate 75 just north of the Tennessee River). The Federals pushed the Confederates back to a hill about a mile from their pontoon bridge, where the Confederates made a stand.[6]

During the rainy and stormy night, Burnside decided to withdraw once again. As the Federals began to move back to Lenoirs on November 15, the Confederates with their troops now across the Tennessee River began to follow. At a point just south of the previously mentioned church, a road (no longer existing) turned toward the Lenoir – Loudon Road (basically modern day Hwy 11). The Federal troops took this road and eventually arrived at Lenoirs. The leading division of Confederates under General Micah Jenkins followed the enemy on this route. The second division of Confederates under General Lafayette McLaws continued up Hotchkiss Valley Road where it ended at the Lenoir-Eaton Crossroads Road (present day Old Highway 95) and was ordered to camp there for the night.

During the night of November 15-16, Burnside ordered all of his troops to withdraw toward Knoxville. Some troops and supplies were put on the only available train and proceeded to Knoxville. The rest of the troops were forced to march to Knoxville. Because of recent heavy rains, the roads were in horrible condition, which made progress very slow. Burnside had sent Colonel Charles G. Loring, his Assistant Inspector General, to 'reconnoiter the ground near Campbell's Station'. Burnside was 'satisfied' that his forces 'would have to make dispositions there to check the enemy until night'.[7]

Near daylight on November 16, the Confederates under General Jenkins began to move toward Lenoirs only to find the enemy gone.

---

[6] Gerald L. Augustus, *The Loudon County Area of East Tennessee in the War 1861-1865* (Paducah, KY: Turner Publishing Company, 2000), pp. 68-72.

[7] *The War of Rebellion*, Series 1, Volume 31, Part 1, p. 274.

The Confederates slowed up to plunder the 80 to 100 wagons of supplies left by Burnside's men. These wagons were supposed to have been destroyed by the Union troops before leaving but had been left with minimum or no damage. At the urging of their officers, the Confederates followed the retreating Union troops. Colonel John Bratton's South Carolina Brigade of Jenkins' Division began the pursuit with the 5th South Carolina Infantry commanded by Lieutenant Colonel John D. Wylie in the lead.[8]

About 8.00 am Longstreet sent orders for McLaws' men, who were camped at the north end of the Hotchkiss Valley Road, to proceed out to the Kingston Road (present day Hwy 70) and cut off the Union forces before they could get to Campbell's Station. McLaws in a letter to his wife said that he had his men on the move to Campbell's Station within five minutes of Longstreet's order. McLaws men pushed and only made one stop 'for a few minutes' to allow his division to close up ranks.[9]

In a letter written in March 1864, General Lafayette McLaws claims that General Longstreet's biggest mistake of the East Tennessee Campaign occurred on 15 November 1863. McLaws' exact words stated:

> If Genl Longstreet was in pursuit of the enemy it was not possible to bring him to an engagement by turning towards Lenoir Station, at the time he did, but he could have done so most effectually by pushing on six or seven miles to where there was a road that led to the RR and gave a strong position. This could have been done by dark or a little after without difficulty or he could have marched ahead of the enemy to Campbell's Station.[10]

McLaws and Longstreet had already developed their difficulties by the time McLaws wrote this letter. A close friend and supporter of Longstreet, E. Porter Alexander, his Chief of Artillery, also supported McLaws position. Years after the War, Alexander wrote: 'Had we had good maps of the country, we had it in our power to

---

[8] *The War of Rebellion*, Series 1, Volume 31, Part 1, p. 525.

[9] Augustus, *The Loudon County Area of East Tennessee in the War 1861-1865*, pp. 69-76; *The War of Rebellion*, Series 1, Volume 31, Part 1, p. 482.

[10] John C. Oeffinger (ed.), *A Soldier's General: The Civil War Letters of Major General Lafayette McLaws* (Chapel Hill, NC: The University of North Carolina Press, 2002), pp. 220-21.

have cut off & captured a part of his troops, by pushing directly to Campbell's Station from our crossing; but, instead, we turned towards Lenoir. We arrived too late to attack & during the night the enemy retreated."[11]

Burnside's troops had left Lenoirs on the Lenoir Road (present day Martel Road. Modern day Highway 11 between Lenoir City and Dixie-Lee Junction did not exist in 1863). The Lenoir Road paralleled the railroad for a few miles and then turned to the northeast. Evidently a mounted force was the first to leave. The wagons guarded by the 79th New York (Highlanders) Infantry were next. Colonel John F. Hartranft's 2nd Division of the 9th Corps consisting of the brigades of Colonel Joshua K. Siegfried and Lt. Colonel Edwin Schall followed the wagons. The last to leave was the 1st Division of the 9th Corps commanded by Brigadier General Edward Ferrero, consisting of brigades of Colonel David Morrison, Colonel Benjamin C. Christ, and Colonel William B. Humphrey. Humphrey's was the last brigade to leave at about 7.00 am. The 20th Michigan was in the lead of Humphrey's brigade followed by the 2nd Michigan, and the rearguard was the 17th Michigan Infantry. Humphrey's regiments only averaged a little over 200 men each. The brigade was supported by two cannons from Jacob Roemer's 34th New York Battery.[12]

The 100th Pennsylvania Infantry was a member of this brigade, but on this day it was on detached duty. Seven companies were sent with the wagons as guards and had no part in the coming battle. Companies A, D, and F, under the command of Captain Thomas J. Hamilton, had been involved in destroying supplies at Lenoirs and were traveling ahead of Humphrey's brigade. With the impending battle, the three companies stopped at Campbell's Station and were

---

[11] Edward Porter Alexander, *Fighting for the Confederacy: The Personal Recollections of General Edward Porter Alexander* (Chapel Hill, NC: The University of North Carolina Press, 1989), pp. 315-16.

[12] William Henry Brearley, *Recollections of the East Tennessee Campaign* (Detroit, MI: Tribune Book and Job Office, 1871), pp. 16-17; *The War of Rebellion*, Series 1, Volume 31, Part 1, p. 350; Summer Carruth, *History of the Thirty-Fifth Regiment, Massachusetts, Volunteers* (Boston, MA: Mills, Knight & Co., Printers, 1884), p. 180; John Robertson (compiler), *Michigan in the War* (Revised Edition; Lansing, MI: W.S. George & Company, 1882), p. 11.

assigned to Christ's Brigade until they rejoined Humphrey's Brigade when it finally arrived.[13]

During the confusion of withdrawing during the night, two companies of Burnside's force at Lenoirs did not receive the order to retreat. One of these units was Company G, 112th Illinois Mounted Infantry under the command of 1st Lieutenant Thomas E. Milchrist. On 15 November they had been ordered by Brigadier General Robert B. Potter, commander of the 9th Corps, to rest and await orders. Evidently General Potter had forgotten to send the orders, and they did not realize the army had retreated until they came under attack from the Confederates on the morning of the 16th. Company G escaped with the loss of one man mortally wounded and three men captured. Two of the captured men died while prisoners of war.

Company G finally reached the rest of Burnside's forces at Campbell's Station. There they learned why they had been ordered to remain until further orders. They had been designated to be an escort for General Burnside but somehow had not received the orders. At Campbell's Station they received their orders and served as dispatch carriers during the ensuing battle.[14]

Until about 9.00 am on the wet, cold morning of the 16th of November, little fighting had taken place. There had been some long range skirmishing along the road with no reported casualties from gun fire. There were casualties of another kind just prior to the beginning of the Battle of Campbell's Station. Company B of the 111th Ohio Infantry under command of Lieutenant Omar P. Norris had been on picket duty during the night of 15-16 November at Lenoirs Station. Due to the 'negligence of the officer in charge of the pickets', the Lieutenant and fifty-two of his command had not been notified that Burnside's Army had retreated toward Knoxville. On the

---

[13] William Gilfillan Gavin, *Campaigning With the Roundheads: The History of the Hundredth Pennsylvania Veteran Volunteer Infantry Regiment in the American Civil War 1861-1865* (Dayton, OH: Morningside House, Inc., 1989), pp. 331-33.

[14] Bradford F. Thompson, *History of the 112th Regiment of Illinois Volunteer Infantry in the Great War of the Rebellion 1862-1865* (Toulon, IL: The Stark County News Office, 1885), pp. 131-32. Private John E. McMillan the wounded soldier did not die until January 1864 in Knoxville. Of the captured, Private William W. Starboard was wounded and exchanged 20 November 1864; Privates Andrew P. Folk and Ransom D. Foster both died in Andersonville, Georgia Prisoner of War Camp.

morning of the 16th, Norris and his men found themselves behind Southern lines. Company B was able to reach the railroad and had almost reunited with the rest of their army at Campbell's Station, when they were surrounded and captured.[15]

As they moved back toward Campbell's Station, the 17th Michigan came upon a Federal cook sitting on a log by the side of the road. The cook, smoking a pipe, had all sorts of pans and kettles tied on his body. The Michigan troops told him that he had better get moving as they were the last Federal troops leaving Lenoirs. He replied, 'I'm not afraid; I am an old soldier.' The 17th moved on and left the old soldier sitting. Shortly after getting out of sight of the cook, the 17th Michigan heard a shot in the direction they had just left. The next thing they heard was the clanking pots and pans. They soon saw the old soldier running toward them. He passed through their lines, kept running and was next seen by the Michigan soldiers in Knoxville.[16]

The entire Lenoir Road used by the troops consisted of nothing but East Tennessee red clay, and after days of rain it had been churned into a horrible condition. There was much confusion and delays as the Union troops edged toward the Kingston Road.

Where present day Martel Road goes under the railroad, the Lenoir Road veered to the northeast and continued to present day Kingston Pike where it intersected with that road at present day First Baptist Church.[17]

Near the junction of the Lenoir Road with Kingston Road, three caissons belonging to 34th New York Artillery (a.k.a. Company L, New York Heavy Artillery and Roemer's Battery) were stuck in the mud. Captain Jacob Roemer, the commander of the company, accompanied two of his four 3 inch rifled cannons ahead of the caissons in Morrison's Brigade. The remaining two cannons of Roemer's Battery were with Humphrey's Brigade at the end of the column. When Roemer went to help extract the caissons, he found Sergeant J.J. Johnston throwing ammunition down the hill. Roemer

---

[15] *The War of Rebellion*, Series 1, Volume 31, Part 1, p. 391.

[16] Brearley, *Recollections of the East Tennessee Campaign*, pp. 18-19.

[17] Digby G. Seymour, *Divided Loyalties: Fort Sanders and the Civil War in East Tennessee* (Rev. Ed.; Knoxville, TN: East Tennessee Historical Society, 1982), pp. 229-30.

Figure 4
**The Ordeal of Moving the Cannon at Night through Rain and Mud**
(Harper's Weekly, 21 November 1863, p. 741)

wanted to know what Johnston was doing and why. Johnston replied that General Burnside had seen the stuck caissons and told him to empty the chest to lighten the load. Roemer ordered the Sergeant to stop the destruction of ammunition and wait for Roemer's return. When General Burnside was found, Roemer explained the dire need for every piece of ammunition. Burnside told Roemer that the horses, caissons, and ammunition would be lost if weight was not reduced. Just then a herd of harnessed mules that had been brought up from Lenoirs Station appeared, and the solution to the problem was solved. Burnside happily ordered the mules to aid in moving the heavy ammunition which would be needed in the fight to come.[18]

---

[18] Jacob Roemer, *Reminiscences of the War of the Rebellion, 1861-1865* (Flushing, NY: Estate of Jacob Roemer, 1897), pp. 159-60.

# 3

## 'THE BALL IS OPENED'

As the Federals retreated toward Campbell's Station, Company B, South Carolinian Palmetto Sharpshooters, acting as skirmishers for the regiment, pushed forward until they neared the present day intersection of Virtue and Evans Roads. The Lenoir-Campbell's Station road ran approximately parallel with and to the north of the present day Evans Road. Just north of and in the vicinity of the Virtue Cemetery, Companies G, E, and K of the 17th Michigan were ordered to stop and slow up the advancing Confederates. The rest of their regiment was to form on the western bank of Little Turkey Creek (In all reports and regimental histories this stream was referred to as Turkey Creek. What is now named North Turkey Creek and Turkey Creek were unnamed streams or creeks). The 17th Michigan was to allow the rest of their brigade time to cross the creek and move up the long hill on the other side. [See Map 2 below.]

In front of the three 17th Michigan companies was a large open field 400 yards wide that ran past them to the creek behind them. The Confederates had stopped in the woods at the edge of the field. Company E was stretched out across the road with G and K in reserve a little closer to the creek. As soon as the Confederates began to fire, Company G went to the right and Company K to the left of Company E and formed into a skirmish line. Up to this point there had been no reported casualties; one of the first Southern shots killed a Michigan soldier. Although many of the Southerners' shots went high hitting trees and sounded 'like hail on a roof', soon more casualties occurred.

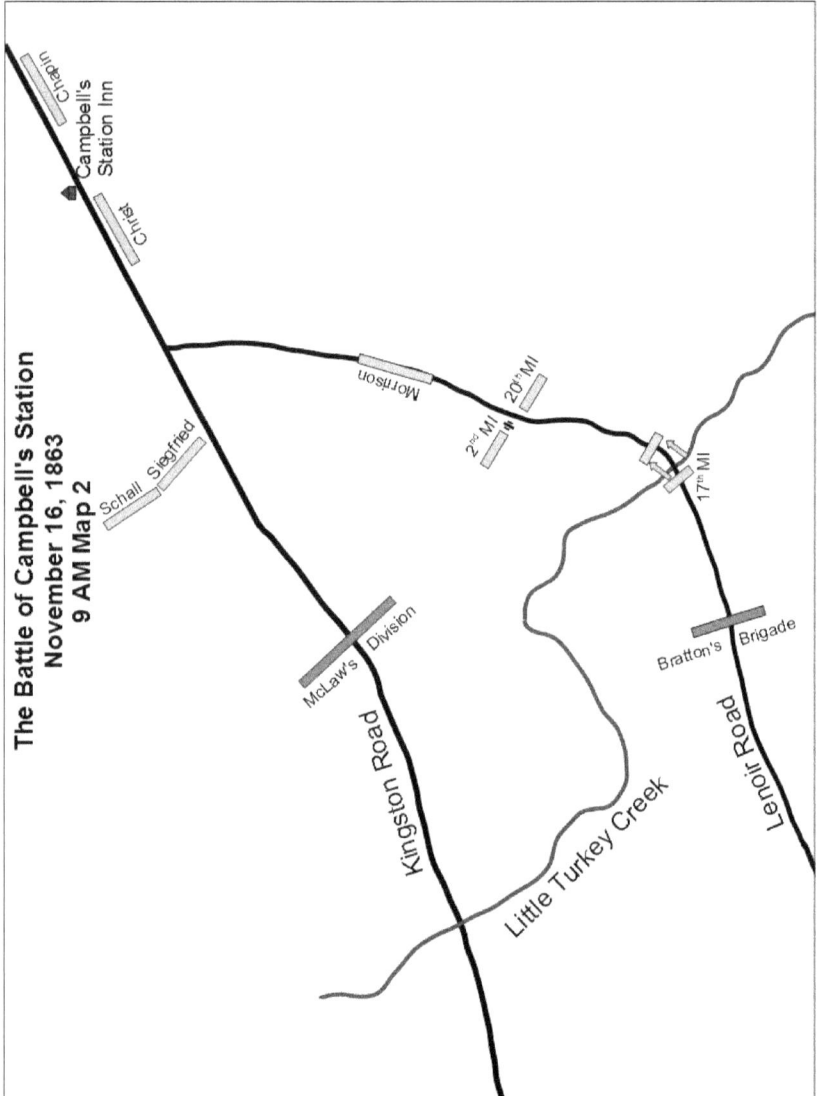

Figure 5
**Map 2 – Battle of Campbell's Station, Early Morning**
(Created by Christopher L. Augustus)

These three companies stood their ground until Confederate troops started to move around both flanks. Then they retreated to the western bank of Little Turkey Creek where the remaining seven companies of the 17th Michigan were formed to face the enemy with the creek at their backs. The road crossed the creek just below a mill, mill dam, and mill pond.[1] [See Map 2.]

Figure 6
*The Old Mill where Some of the 17th Michigan Fought and Were Captured*
(It Is Unclear Whether This Is the Original Mill or a Later Reconstruction on the Site.) From the Farragut Folklife Museum Collections.

General Edward Ferrero, commander of the 1st Division, was near or in Campbell's Station about to sit down to eat breakfast. When he heard the sound of firing, Ferrero, a former dance instructor, was reported to have stood up and announced to everyone within hearing, 'Gentlemen, the ball is opened'.[2]

---

[1] Brearley, *Recollections of the East Tennessee Campaign*, p. 19; Lewis, *Camp Life of a Confederate Boy*, p. 69.

[2] Brearley, *Recollections of the East Tennessee Campaign*, p. 19; Lewis, *Camp Life of a Confederate Boy*, p. 69.

The Confederate attack continued straight toward the 17th Michigan but hesitated at the sight of the whole regiment. When the South Carolinians began to move around both ends of the regiment, the Michiganders began individually to cross the creek. Soon bullets were coming into the 17th from three directions, and the regiment's commander Lt. Colonel Comstock ordered 'About Face' and then 'In Retreat March'.[3]

When the 17th began to cross Little Turkey Creek, a general rout began to take place. In their haste soldiers began throwing backpacks and blankets away. Captain John Tyler, Company G, who had been wounded at the beginning of the fighting, waved his bloody hand and tried to rally the troops but to no avail.

As the 17th Michigan continued up the hill, the United States flag bearer, Sgt. Joseph Brandle, stopped and waved his flag to rally the men to make a stand. He was soon shot twice, once through the right eye and once in the side, but he only gave up the flag when ordered by Lt. Colonel Comstock. Corporal Franklin Knight took the flag next and was almost immediately killed. Then Acting Major Frederick W. Swift took the flag. Swift yelled 'We have fallen back just far enough; we will form here'. Someone asked, 'Who shall we form on' (sic). He replied, 'Form on me!' Enough of the 17th Michigan stopped and were able to make a stand and return fire.[4] Thirty years later, Sergeant Brandle and Major Swift would each receive the Medal of Honor for their deeds just above the creek.[5] [See Map 2.]

The 17th Michigan's stand gave the two other Michigan regiments and the one section of artillery time to form at the top of the hill. The two cannon section was part of the 34th New York Artillery and was under the over all command of 1st Lt. Thomas Heasley. This new line was probably formed near the intersection of present day Midhurst and Carlyle Drives. The 20th Michigan Infantry was on the southeast side of the road commanded by Lt. Colonel William Huntington Smith. The 2nd Michigan Infantry commanded by

---

[3] John Maltman, Bently Historical Museum, http/www.17thmicoe.org/letter.htm, p. 4.

[4] Brearley, *Recollections of the East Tennessee Campaign*, p. 21.

[5] Brearley, *Recollections of the East Tennessee Campaign*, p. 21; W.F. Beyer and O.F. Keydel, *Deeds of Valor: How American's Civil War Heroes Won the Congressional Medal of Honor* (New York, NY: Smithmark Publishers, 2000), pp. 278-79.

Figure 7
*Lieutenant Colonel Frederick W. Swift*
*Awarded Medal of Honor for his Actions at the Battle of Campbell's Station*
From the Farragut Folklife Museum Collections.

Major Cornelius Byington was on the northwest side of the road to support the 34th New York's section of two, three inch rifled cannons (in modern times these are usually referred to as three inch Ordnance Rifles). Thirteen men from the 20th Michigan had earlier been detailed to the artillery in order for that unit to perform adequately.[6] [See Map 2.]

In order to extradite themselves from the Southerners, the remnants of the 17th Michigan charged the closest Confederates who were so surprised at this sudden turn of events, they fell back. The 17th was thus able finally to begin moving up the hill to join the rest of their brigade. When they moved, the artillery could finally fire safely over the heads of the 17th Michigan. The exploding shells caused the Confederates who were coming up to attack the beleaguered 17th Michigan to either slow down or in some cases to retreat.[7]

Some of the 17th Michigan had used the old mill as cover to fight the Southerners. Before they could retreat from the mill, they were surrounded and captured. While Sergeant Morgan Dowling, Company F, one of the men captured in the mill, was held as a prisoner, he observed the following incident. When the first shells began to explode, some of the Confederates ran 'in perfect panic, did not stop till they had re-crossed the creek'. Prior to the shelling, General Longstreet had arrived, crossed to the east side of the creek and was talking to some of the Union prisoners. At that moment the Unionist charged, moved further up the hill, and then the shells began to fly. Longstreet seeing his men falling back gave orders to bring more troops to flank Michiganders. The general remounted his horse and rode away to help hurry more men forward. As soon as Longstreet moved away, one of the New Yorker's shells exploded on the very spot where he had been standing.[8] This was first of two

---

[6] Roemer, *Reminiscences of the War of the Rebellion, 1861-1865*, p. 162; Hewett (ed.), *Supplement to the Official Records of the Union and Confederate Armies*, p. 386; Seymour, *Divided Loyalties*, p. 231; *The War of Rebellion*, Series 1, Volume 31, Part 1, pp. 350, 365, 370-71. No record was found indicating whether the infantrymen were assigned to the first section or were with Lt. Heasley's section.

[7] Brearley, *Recollections of the East Tennessee Campaign*, p. 21.

[8] Brearley, *Recollections of the East Tennessee Campaign*, pp. 21-22.

instances that day in which General James Longstreet could have lost his life.

Figure 8
*17ᵗʰ Michigan Infantry Monument*
(From the Farragut Folklife Museum Collections)
This monument is located in the Virtue Cemetery on Evans Road near the intersection with Virtue Road. This monument was erected in 2002 by the 17th Michigan Volunteer Infantry Regiment Company E, Inc., a reenactment organization.
The hill where the two Medal of Honor recipients earned their awards is unseen and just to the left of the photograph.
The monument reads:
Medal of Honor

17TH Michigan Volunteer
Turkey Creek & Campbell Station
November 16, 1863
9TH Corps, First Division
Third Brigade
Captain Frederick Swift
Sgt. Joseph Brandle

On November 16, 1863, the 17th Michigan
was assigned as part of the Rear Guard
along with the 2nd Michigan, 20th Michigan
and the 100th Pennsylvania to protect the
rest of Burnside's Army which were now
in retreat into the defenses of Knoxville.
Almost cut off, Captain Fredrick Swift
of Company E and Sgt. Joseph Brandle,
the flag bearer, rallied the regiment
and stopped the Confederates from over
running them and the rest of the guard.
For this action, Captain Swift and Sgt.
Brandle were awarded the Medal of Honor.

Losses for the 17TH MICHIGAN
7 Killed
52 Wounded

Private V.W. Bruce, 17th Michigan Infantry, was wounded and captured in this part of the Battle of Campbell's Station. His right leg had to be amputated. He was nursed by a local family and rescued when General William T. Sherman's troops occupied the area in December 1863. [Bruce's entire adventure may be read in Excursus 2, 'The Velorus W. Bruce Story'.]

As the 17th Michigan started up the hill, they were in woods near the creek but came into an open field. Some of the Confederates had made it around the mill pond and were on the west side of the field, as the Michigan men ran up the hill. This caused the survivors to veer to the right and eventually around the left flank of the 20th Michigan and finally regain the road. As the 17th came back into line, the 2nd and 20th Michigan gave them a cheer. The 17th then reformed and moved into line on the left of the 20th Michigan. When the 17th Michigan was in line, Colonel Comstock shouted out 'boys steady – remember you are on Brigade drill now'. The 'boys' did 'steady' and never again during the engagement panic as they had at the creek.[9]

The Confederates, of course, continued to advance and move around the flanks of the Union brigade. Almost as soon as the 17th got into position, Colonel William Huntington Smith of the 20th Michigan was killed instantly from a gunshot wound to the head. Colonel Smith 'expired instantly, without a word or groan, while bravely encouraging the men'. Major Byron M. Cutcheon, Smith's senior officer, immediately took command of the regiment. Fort Huntington Smith, one of the Federals' Knoxville defensive forts, was named for this fallen officer. It was located near present day Welcher and Patterson Streets and has long been leveled.[10]

The 17th Michigan was in line in the open field without any protection. A few yards to their rear, they discovered a wooden rail fence at the edge of a woods. They withdrew behind the fence to await the next attack. The other two regiments saw the advantage of the woods and withdrew to this new line. Using the rails as support for their rifle muskets, they waited. When the Confederate line got quite close, the Michiganders fired which 'threw them into confusion, and before it could be reformed a second volley scattered and drove them back'.[11]

Humphrey's Brigade began pulling back toward the Kingston Road closely followed by the reinforced Confederates. After passing through the woods the brigade came to large open fields near the Kingston Road. In order to cross these fields to rejoin the rest of the army, Humphrey ordered the brigade to attack which drove the Confederates back and allowed the Michiganders to line up with the Morrison's Brigade.[12]

---

[9] Maltman, Bently Historical Museum, p. 4; *The War of Rebellion*, Series 1, Volume 31, Part 1, p. 371; Brearley, *Recollections of the East Tennessee Campaign*, p. 22; Irwin Shepard, 'Letters from Sergeant Irwin Shepard, Co. E, 17th Michigan Infantry', Typescript of the original letters (University of Michigan, Ann Arbor, Michigan, in the files of the Farragut Folklife Museum), 6 December 1863.

[10] Seymour, *Divided Loyalties*, p. 249; *The War of Rebellion*, Series 1, Volume 31, Part 1, pp. 365, 371.

[11] Brearley, *Recollections of the East Tennessee Campaign*, p. 22; Byron Cutcheon, *The Story of the Twentieth Michigan Infantry, July 15th, 1862 to May 30th, 1865* (Lansing, MI: Robert Smith Printing Company, 1904), p. 75.

[12] Brearley, *Recollections of the East Tennessee Campaign*, p. 22; Cutcheon, *The Story of the Twentieth Michigan Infantry, July 15th, 1862 to May 30th, 1865*, p. 75.

One of the two cannon in Lieutenant Thomas Healsey's section of the 34th New York Artillery was under the command of Sergeant John H. Starkins and the other under Sergeant Valentine Rossbach. Captain Jacob Roemer, commander of the 34th New York Artillery, recommended both sergeants to receive the Medal of Honor for their heroic actions in successfully withdrawing and firing their cannons without losing a man. Sergeant Starkins received the Medal of Honor with the citation that he was awarded the medal for his actions at Campbell's Station. Sergeant Rossbach also received the Medal of Honor, but the citation does not mention his action at Campbell's Station. Rossbach's official citation cites his actions at Spotsylvania, Virginia, on 12 May 1864. Since it would have been difficult to award Starkins the medal without awarding Rossbach the same, in essence they both received their medals for actions at Campbell's Station. In the area between Little Turkey Creek and the junction of the Lenoir and Kingston Roads, four Medal of Honor awards were issued.[13] [See Map 3.]

---

[13] Report of Jacob Roemer, New York State Military Museum and Veterans Research Center, http://dmna.ny.gov/historic/reghist/civil/artillery/34thIndBat/34thInd. Civil War Medal of Honor Recipients, http://www.history.army.mil/html/moh/civwarmz.html.

## Excursus 2

## The Velorus W. Bruce Story[14]

'An Adrian Boy'

'V.W. Bruce, who visited old acquaintances here last week, returned to the city Thursday, from a family reunion at the home of his brother Chas. W. Bruce, of Hudson, and he favored a representative of The Telegram with the following interesting reminiscence of his service in the Civil War.

I went out from Adrian College in Company A, Seventeenth Michigan Infantry, August 2, 1862, which regiment was assigned to Burnside's Ninth Army Corps, and was in the Army of the Potomac until the spring of 1863, when we went west into Kentucky, then to Vicksburg, and returning north went into East Tennessee by way of Cincinnati, Lexington and Cumberland Gap, going into winter quarters about 25 miles west of Knoxville, where we built neat log shanties.

On the night of November 15 we were aroused at midnight and ordered to pack up and get ready to march immediately, and burn our shanties. The late order made us very indignant for we thought we were comfortably settled for the winter. But Longstreet had withdrawn his corps from the Confederate army before Chattanooga and started for East Tennessee, and we went to the Tennessee River, near Loudon, on the 14th to prevent his crossing. On arriving there we received orders from Gen. Grant to fall back from (sic) Knoxville and fortify and hold that city and he would send a force up in Longstreet's rear. Before daylight on the morning of the 15th we had commenced said retreat, and at sundown reached Lenoir Station, where we burned our shanties. The Confederate forces were close upon us, and were halted and sent into camp for the night by a shot from one of our cannons. Our regiment was imme-

---

[14] This account is taken from an undated newspaper article that was published in *The Telegram* newspaper of Adrian, Michigan, sometime after 1888. A transcript of the article and addition information is in the files of the Farragut Folklife Museum.

diately thrown out as pickets, and the night was a sleepless one for us.

Figure 9
*'United We Stand'*
*Post War Photograph of Velorus W. Bruce and Frank M. Howe*

On the morning of the 16th the pickets were ordered in about daylight, and we found our regiment rear guard for the day, supported by our brigade, and the balance of Burnside's force was well on the way to Knoxville. We cut down the wheels and set fire to three or four of our supply wagons, which we could not take with us, and started on after our army. On reaching Turkey Creek, about eight miles from Lenoir Station, the Johnnies overtook us and Company A, with one or two other companies, were deployed as skirmishers, and while falling back across creek we filled our canteens with fresh water. On ascending the bank of the creek I was wounded through the knee joint of my right leg and immediately fell into the hands of the enemy. A dozen or fifteen other comrades were wounded at the same time one being Israel Mapes of Company A, and Corporal Knight and Ezekiel Sargeant of the same company were killed. Knight receiving his death wound in the forehead while carrying the colors, and Sargeant, dying unconscious from his wound in the breast, lying beside me and touching elbows during the following night.

While lying on the field, wounded, I feared that my foot would swell and make it difficult to get my boot off, after my wound became sore, therefore, I held my foot to one of the Confederates who came along, and asked him to pull off my boot. He stopped, laid down his gun, pulled off my boot, handed it to me, picked up his gun and went on.

Soon after the above incident, I noticed a company of Confederates coming across the creek and filling their canteens with fresh water, and I noticed that one had a cedar canteen, made of staves, heads and hoops like a barrel. I wanted such a one to send home as a relic, therefore I kept my eye on this Confederate, and when he came along I stumped him for a trade, and there, lying on the field wounded, traded canteens, and now have the much coveted relic at my home in Big Rapids [Michigan].

We laid on the field until dark, when some of our own comrades, who had been captured, but not wounded, came under rebel guard and carried us all to a farm house, just across the road from where we fell. The farm was owned by a loyal Union widow, Mrs. Nancy S. Galbraith, who had two sons in our army in the First Tennessee Infantry. She also had at home four small children and daughter 18 years old. This widow gave up to us the best room in her house, and on the following day the daughter, with a neighbor woman, went with ropes and brought bundles of straw on their backs a mile and a half to make beds for us wounded boys to lie on. Bed ticks were filled and laid in rows on each side of the room, with an alley-way between to the large fireplace. Our wounds were dressed and my leg amputated by the Confederate surgeons, just 24 hours after we were wounded, and two of Mrs. Galbraith's boys, Abram and David, buried my foot in the back yard.

We remained there nearly a month, and Mrs. Galbraith furnished from her own secreted stores all we had to eat during our stay there, except one ration of flour which the Confederates gave us, and she and her older daughter did our cooking and washing, and took care of us as our mothers and sisters would have done if they had had the opportunity.

On Thanksgiving night the young women of the neighborhood dropped in to make our Thanksgiving a memorable one. It was a surprise visit, and they brought a large dish of molasses candy with them, and passed it to us boys as we sat up in bed, and we had a genuine candy pull in Dixie on that Thanksgiving night in 1863.

Sherman's forces finally came up in Longstreet's rear and hustled the latter out so fast that he could not take us with him, hence we were recaptured and taken to Knoxville hospitals. When I fell, wounded, and my comrades could not carry me off the field, and could only judge of the nature of my wound from my appearance as they saw me fall. Lieutenant C.D. Todd wrote home to his folks that Bruce was mortally wounded and left in the hands of the Rebels. This news was immediately conveyed to my folks and was the last they heard of me until after I was recaptured. They gave me up for dead, and President McEldowney announced my death in chapel exercises and pronounced quite an obituary, but I lived to surprise them all and spent three years in school at the college after the war. My first letter, after I was wounded, was to my mother and she received it on Christmas eve, and she assured me that it was the merriest Christmas of her whole life – the dead was alive, the lost was found.

I returned home on a furlough and received my discharge from the army at St. Mary's hospital in Detroit, March 27, 1864, and on returning home was presented with the money ($100) to procure an artificial limb, a patriotic gift from the citizens of Adrian. I immediately went to Cincinnati and procured the limb.

Soon after I returned home, I made application to the government for compensation for Mrs. Galbraith, for the provisions she furnished us and the care she and her family gave us during our fortunate stay in her house. At the request of the government I furnished proofs substantiating the claim, and about two weeks after furnishing the proofs, received a letter from the daughter, Miss Laurinda, informing me that they had just received $357 from the government for taking care of us boys. It was a surprise to them, coming just in the nick of time, when they were wondering where their next meal was coming from. I had not informed them of my step in their behalf.

I visited the family just 25 years after I was wounded, and had a most royal visit with the children, the sainted mother having gone to her reward in heaven three or four years before.'

Nancy Serena Galbraith (1819-1884) was the widow of Samuel Gaston Galbraith (1813-1857). Her two sons in the Union Army were Samuel Andrew, who was born in 1844, and Thomas Galbraith, who was born in 1846. Both brothers served in Company D, 3rd Tennessee Infantry, not the 1st Tennessee as stated by Bruce. Mrs. Galbraith's other children were Lourinda Jane, born in 1848, David R., born in 1850, Abram L., born 1852, Ann Eliza, born in 1856, and Matthew Gaston, born in 1858, months after his father's death.

# 4

## ACTION AT THE JUNCTION

While Humphrey's Brigade had fought hard to slow the Confederates under General Jenkins, the rest of Burnside's army had by very hard marching reached the junction of the Kingston and Lenoir Roads. Some participants estimated that the Union army had won the race to the junction by as little as fifteen minutes. Confederate General Lafayette McLaws' division had camped near the junction of the Hotckiss Valley Road and the Lenoir-Eaton Road on the night of 15-16 November. McLaws received orders from General James Longstreet at 8.00 am to march on the Kingston Road to Campbell's Station. McLaws stated that his troops were on the move within five minutes of receiving the order. According to Longstreet, he did not order McLaws to 'double quick' his march to Campbell's Station. Longstreet's plan was that McLaws could either continue up to Campbell's Station and reach there ahead of the Union troops or be brought across from the Kingston Road to attack Burnside in the flank.[1] Of course, this plan did not come to pass.

A Confederate cavalry brigade, temporarily under the command of Colonel John R. Hart, preceded McLaws' Infantry Division on the Kingston Road. This cavalry brigade was composed of the 1$^{st}$, 3$^{rd}$, 4$^{th}$, 6$^{th}$ Georgia Cavalry and Captain Jannedine H. Wiggins' Arkansas Battery. Most of the Confederate cavalry under the com-

---

[1] James Longstreet, *From Manassas to Appomattox: Memoirs of the Civil War in America* (Bloomington, IN: Indiana University Press, 1960 reprint of 1896 edition); Lafayette McLaws, *A Soldier's General: The Civil War Letters of Major General Lafayette McLaws* (Chapel Hill, NC: The University of North Carolina Press, 2002), p. 221.

mand of General Joseph Wheeler had previously been sent on the other side of the river to try to capture the hills which overlooked Knoxville. The day prior to the Battle of Campbell's Station, Wheeler's cavalry had fired on the Union forts which guarded that approach. These forts sat on high hills and were defended with infantry and many cannons. He wisely chose not to make an all out attack with cavalry and rode south from Knoxville to find a crossing of the Holston River to rejoin Longstreet.[2] [See Map 1.]

Meanwhile, the rest of Burnsides' Army had finally reached the junction of the Lenoir and Kingston Roads at about 9.00 am. The first Union troops to arrive were the cavalry under the command of Colonel James Biddle of the 6th Indiana Cavalry. He had about 200 of his men plus the 8th Michigan Cavalry Regiment under the command of Major Henry C. Edgerly. This cavalry force was sent down the road toward Kingston, and after they had gone about two and a half miles, Biddle's command found Hart's Confederate cavalry which was in advance of Confederate General McLaws' Infantry Division. The Union cavalry was successful in driving the Confederates back to their infantry support. The 8th Michigan Cavalry was armed with seven shot Spencer Carbines, and the 6th Indiana was armed with single shot Burnside Carbines. As the Confederate infantry came into the fight, Biddle's cavalry force would then slowly retreat back along the Kingston Road to its infantry support near the Lenoir Road junction. This cavalry action gave the Union infantry time to deploy into a line of battle.[3] [See Excursus 3 for an interesting story of the Lost Rifle that occurred at this time in the battle.] [See Map 3 – The Battle of Campbell's Station, November 16, 1863, Noon.]

---

[2] Longstreet, *From Manassas to Appomattox*, p. 487; Edward G. Longacre, *A Soldier to the Last: Maj. Gen. Joseph Wheeler in Blue and Gray* (Washington, DC: Potomac Books, Inc., 2007), p. 130; J.W. Minnich, 'How Some History Is Written', *Confederate Veteran Magazine*, Volume XIII, Number 3 March 1905 (Wilmington, NC: Broadfoot Publishing Company, 1988), p. 11; Stewart Sifakis, *Compendium of the Confederate Armies: Florida and Arkansas* (New York, NY: Facts On File, 1992), p. 38.

[3] *The War of Rebellion*, Series 1, Volume 31, Part 1, pp. 274, 333; Samuel Wells, *Autobiography of Samuel Wells* (New Carlisle, IN: Gazette Printing Company, 1897), p. 8; James G. Genco (compiler), *Arming Michigan's Regiments 1862-1864* (J.G. Genco, 1982), p. 103; William J. Bolton, Richard A. Sauers (ed.), *The Civil War Journal of Colonel William J. Bolton, 51st Pennsylvania, April 20, 1861 – August 2, 1865* (Conshohocken, PA: Combined Publishing, 2000), p. 150.

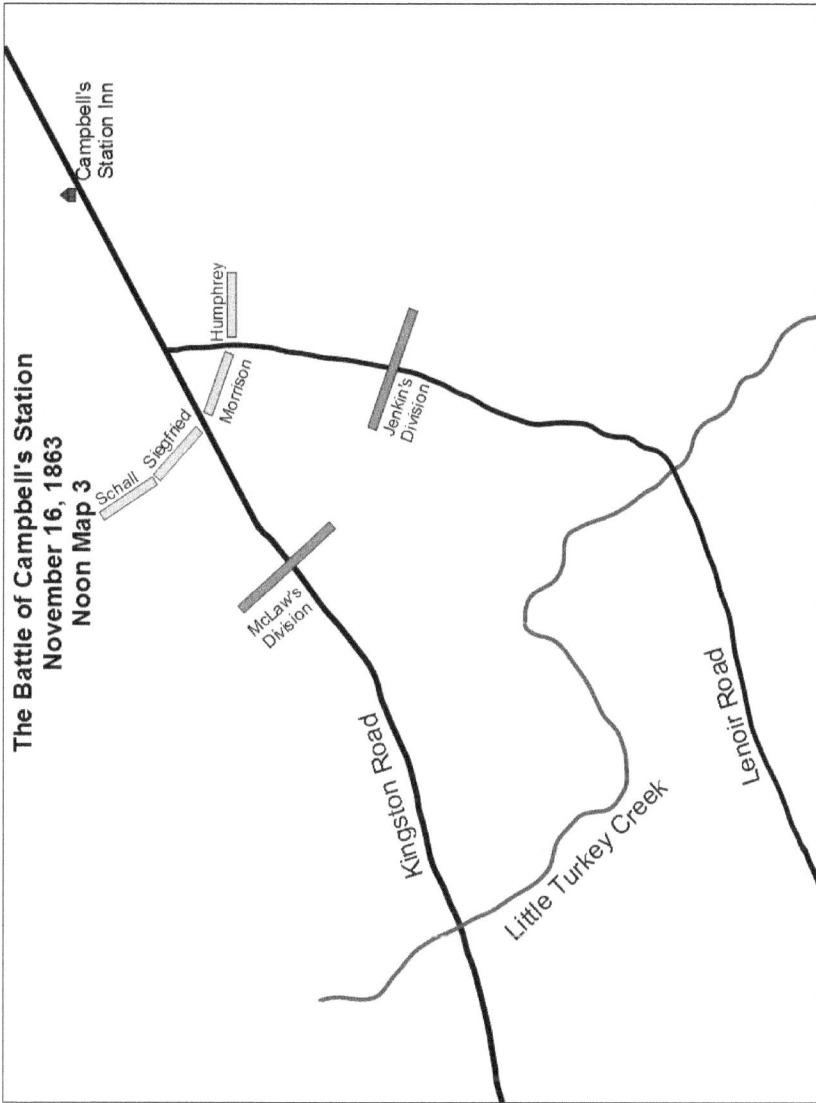

Figure 10
*Map 3 – Action at the Junction. Noon.*
Created by Christopher L. Augustus

The land near the junction of the roads was generally heavily wooded north of the road, but there was about a six acre field near the intersection of the two roads. The land south of the Kingston Road in this area was generally cleared fields.

Next, Union Colonel John F. Hartranft's Infantry Division, consisting of two brigades under the command of Colonel Joshua K. Siegfried and Lt. Colonel Edwin Schall and Companies L and M (Consolidated) 3rd U.S. Artillery, reached the Kingston Road behind the cavalry. Instead of continuing on to Knoxville, Hartranft's two brigades and one section (two cannons) of the artillery turned left onto the Kingston Road. On this day these two brigades were even smaller than usual. Colonel Siegfried's contained only the 2nd Maryland and the 48th Pennsylvania. The 21st Massachusetts of this brigade had been sent on with the wagons and stopped to support the artillery that had gone into position at the intersection of the Kingston and Concord Roads. As wagons and more artillery came to the intersection, they moved to the right on the Kingston Road toward Knoxville.

Lt. Colonel Schall's Brigade had only the 35th Massachusetts and 51st Pennsylvania. The 11th New Hampshire, usually a member of Schall's brigade, had been stationed in Knoxville during this battle. After traveling a short distance west on the Kingston Road, the brigades of Siegfried and Schall went into line of battle north of the Kingston Road. Colonel Biddle's cavalry after their attack took up position on the right of Hartranft's line. According to Hartranft, he 'had considerable trouble to hold the cavalry on that flank'.[4]

Hartranft's troops were followed by Colonel Marshall W. Chapin's Brigade of the 23rd Corps. These troops, who had seen heavy duty at Huff's Ferry against Longstreet's Confederates crossing of the Tennessee River, were sent to the east on the Kingston Road. They stopped beyond the Campbell's Station Inn slightly west of

---

[4] *The War of Rebellion*, Series 1, Volume 31, Part 1, p. 333. Summer Carruth, *History of the Thirty-Fifth Regiment, Massachusetts, Volunteers* (Boston, MA: Mills, Knight & Co., Printers, 1884), p. 181; Leander W. Cogswell, *A History of the Eleventh New Hampshire Regiment Volunteer Infantry in the Rebellion War, 1861-1865* (Memphis, TN: General Books, 2010), pp. 74-75, 93, 105-106; Oliver C. Bosbyshell, *The 48th in the War: Being a Narrative of the Campaigns of the 48th Regiment, Infantry, Pennsylvania Veteran Volunteers during the War of the Rebellion* (Philadelphia, PA: Avil Print Company, 1895), p. 132; A.M. Gambone, *Major-General John Frederick Hartranft: Citizen Soldier and Pennsylvania Statesman* (Baltimore, MD: Butternut and Blue, 1995), p. 84.

the Dr. William Nelson Home on the Kingston Road and went into line of battle across the Kingston Road.[5] [See Map 3.]

On arriving at the junction of the Kingston Road, Colonel Benjamin C. Christ's Brigade also turned toward Campbell's Station. They proceeded on until they stopped and went into position to help defend the artillery on the north side of the Kingston Road in the vicinity of the junction of the Concord Road.[6]

The next union troops to arrive at the junction were Colonel David Morrison's Brigade. They took up position between the Kingston and Lenoir Roads in an open field. The 36th Massachusetts Infantry's right was on the Kingston Road. The 8th Michigan Infantry was to the left of the 36th Massachusetts with their left on the Lenoir Road. The 45th Pennsylvania Infantry was in front of the brigade acting as skirmishers. The 79th New York, which was also a part of this brigade, had been sent with the artillery and wagons to the junction of the Concord and Kingston Roads.[7]

Hart's Confederate cavalry could see the Federal troops deploying ahead of them and watched as they went into line of battle. They could also see that even more troops were moving up the Lenoir Road about half a mile to their right. If the cavalry had attacked the Hartranft-Morrison line, they could have been attacked from the rear by Humphrey's Brigade. One Confederate humorously related that their 'policy was to let them (Humphrey's Brigade) go by quietly, since they appeared disposed to be decent'.[8]

The brigades of Siegfried, Schall, and Morrison were soon engaged with General McLaws' Confederate infantry that had advanced on the Kingston Road. The Confederates were able to get close enough to the Union position to fire on General Hartranft and his staff, but none of the Union officers were injured. In the

---

[5] Arthur J and Margaret S. Bush, *Black Power to Black Gold: The life and Times of William E. Hobson* (Bowling Green, KY: A.J. and M.S. Bush, 1990), pp. 41-42; *The War of Rebellion*, Series 1, Volume 31, Part 1, p. 384.

[6] *The War of Rebellion*, Series 1, Volume 31, Part 1, p. 358.

[7] Philip Grenville Woodward, 'The Siege of Knoxville', in *Military Order of the Loyal Legion of the United States*, Volume 30 (Wilmington, NC: Broadfoot Publishing Company, 1992), p. 358; Allen D. Albert (ed.), *History of the Forty-Fifth Regiment Pennsylvania Veteran Volunteer Infantry 1861-1865* (Williamsport, PA: Grit Publishing Company, 1912), p. 93.

[8] J.W. Minnich, 'The Cavalry At Knoxville', *Confederate Veteran Magazine* 13.1, January 1924 (Wilmington, NC: Broadfoot Publishing Company, 1988), p. 11.

meantime, the Union wagons and artillery were still moving up the hills on the Lenoir Road. Colonel Humphrey's Brigade was still the rear guard of the Union army on the Lenoir Road fighting Confederate General Jenkins' aggressive troops. At about 10.00 am Humphrey's Brigade finally reached the left flank of Colonel Morrison's Brigade. This meant that all the wagons and artillery had finally passed onto the Kingston Road and were moving toward Knoxville. Humphrey's men fell into place next to Morrison's regiments. Colonel Morrison 'mounted on a snow white horse, and forming a most conspicuous mark, seemed omnipresent at all points along the brigade line, and added, by his presence, not a little to the steadiness of the troops'. The Union position extended from north of the Kingston Road across the Lenoir Road and south beyond there.[9]

---

[9] *The War of Rebellion*, Series 1, Volume 31, Part 1, pp. 333, 351; Brearley, *Recollections of the East Tennessee Campaign*, p. 22; Frank Moore (ed.), *The Rebellion Record: A Diary of American Events*, Volume 11 (New York, NY: Arno Press, 1977 reprint), p. 11.

## Excursus 3

### The Lost Rifle

The following story was related by Private J.W. Minnich of Company G, 6th Georgia Cavalry. The spelling has been corrected due to the source's often misspelling.

'We followed their (Union) retreating cavalry up the Kingston and Knoxville road, but did not get in range of them until they halted at the junction of the Kingston and Lenoir and Loudon roads, near a large brick house, Campbell's. There they decided to make a stand, though only few in numbers, and as we came in range – a long one – they opened on us. We filed off to the left and formed a line on an eminence above and below a farm house and barn, with our battery (Wiggins) in the center, and began exchanging compliments and the time of day. They appeared to have been armed with short range carbines, and their fire was ineffective, as we had but one man in my company wounded by a spent ball. But it hit him the pit of the stomach and raised an ugly lump without actually breaking the skin. But Bob was a very sick boy for a while.

We had better guns, 'imported Enfields' mostly, with a sprinkling of captured guns of all brands, which proved more effective in combination with our two three-inch Parrotts and smoothbore twelve-pound Napoleon, and induced our friends to withdraw out of sight; we did not follow. Why, we did not know at the time, but shortly afterwards we learned the reason for our not pushing farther forward at that time.

The firing having ceased on both sides, and being of an inquisitive turn of mind, I ventured across the road and crossed a field beyond toward the Lenoir and Loudon road. There was a fence about midway between the two roads (Kingston and Loudon), and a large cherry tree near the fence, in which a gap had been made by cavalry, as the hoofprints clearly indicated. I made for the gap, going up hill, and was surprised to see a long column of bluecoats emerge from the woods down the road to my right and form in line to the left of the road. One, two, three, four, five, and so on until at least 10,000 men, as near as I could judge, debouched into the field and formed in column of regiments, advancing rapidly toward Campbell's Station, less than quarter of mile from where I stood.

Here, then, was the explanation and reason for our not moving on Campbell's Station. After the cavalry had disappeared up the road, seeing that I would impede their march, I turned toward my own command and, in retracing my way through the gap in the fence, happened to glance to the right, when I saw the butt of a gun only slightly protruding from beneath the briars that grew in the fence corners. Without a moment's hesitation, I stooped and picked it up, looking around to discover, if possible, the owner. No one was in sight anywhere near. I called: 'Hello, there!' Receiving no answer, I examined my new acquisition – 'capture' – more closely, and found that it was a rifle such as I had never before seen, and undoubtedly a formidable weapon. Heavy (I judged about thirteen pounds weight), more deeply grooved than any gun I had ever seen, of smaller caliber than any of our guns, and it was sighted for 2,200 yards. 'Gee whillikins! (sic) Why that is one and quarter miles!' Some sharpshooter's gun, I surmised and the owner has been captured or killed. Well, I have his gun anyhow.

I didn't have time to examine the arm in all its aspects, as the bluecoats were advancing very rapidly across the field and road, being then less than a quarter of a mile distant. In fact, they seemed to be in a hurry. Longstreet's men were following rather too close for comfort and in greater numbers. Their business was to keep going. I started down the hill with my own gun slung over my back and carrying my capture on my right shoulder, and was 'making tracks' toward my command, now in full view of the retreating Federals, who paid no attention to it, seemingly at least, but rolled on across the field and disappeared beyond Campbell's house. While they passed with easy range of our battery, and even of our rifles, not a shot was fired from either side; why? I had almost arrived at the Kingston road when I heard behind me a call, repeated several times, to which at first, I paid no attention; but at last, I turned to see who was yelling, 'Hey, hey there!' with such insistence, and found I was being pursued on the run by a 'grayback' like myself, waving his hat and yelling: 'Hey there! You've got my gun.' Stopping short, I waited, till he caught up with me, when almost out breath, he repeated: 'You've got my gun.' I demanded proof. 'Where did you lose it?' He replied: 'I didn't lose it at all – when I got to that cherry tree, I found I was ahead of the Yankees. They were coming up both roads, and I found myself ahead of their cavalry, but between two troops, and I thought I was a goner. But I determined they should not get my gun, so I pushed it under the briars there by the tree, hopped over the fence, and ran along it some distance, and then got back on this side and crawled under the briars in a fence corner and lay here until they had passed by. I don't know whether or not they saw me before I hopped the fence. You fellows were pushing them pretty close (which was a fact), and I guess they were looking back oftener than ahead; but they cut across the field to join the others coming up the Loudon road and went through the fence at the tree. I was afraid some them would see my gun and get it, and that would have put me in a fix.' He then told me it was a 'Whitworth Rifle,' English make, and that 'they cost $1,200 each; that there were 'only twenty of them in Longstreet's Corps' in the hands of sharpshooters only, who were exempt from the usual soldier's routine – guard mounts, drills, etc. – and that every man of them acted on his own free will when there was anything doing, without restraint, subject only to orders from the division commander or Longstreet himself.

He showed me the cartridges, the ball over an inch long, with a powder charge of near three inches in length. Though it was a muzzle-loader, its range was beyond any gun I had ever handled. I could do no better than return the gun to its owner, but how I hated to give it up. I offered to trade my long Enfield for it and give him 'boot'. 'Good Lord, boy! I wouldn't dare go back to camp without my gun. I'd be court-martialed and shot if I lost it that way.' Sound reason for keeping it, I admitted, and at the same time became aware of how very foolish my offer to swap must have sounded to him, as it did to me later.

We walked down to Kingston road, quite near by then, and there we parted, he going toward the rear, while I rejoined my command at the farm house, up the lane west of the road and watched the Union troops pass on up the road, paying no attention to us.'[10]

---

[10] J.W. Minnich, 'Famous Rifles', *Confederate Veteran* XXX Volume 7 July 1922, (Wilmington, North Carolina: Broadfoot Publishing Company, 1988), pp. 247-47.

The muzzle loaded Whitworth Rifles were made in Manchester, England, and imported to the Confederacy in very small numbers. There is no record found that they were purchased by the United States. The barrel length most often was thirty-three inches, but some were thirty-six and even thirty-nine inches. Several different types of sights have been noted on Confederate Whitworths. Some even had scopes which were mounted on the left side of the barrel instead of on top as modern rifles. The Whitworth described in the above account evidently was not fitted for a scope since no mention is made of this feature.

The barrel was .451 caliber and was not round inside with the rifling grooves cut into the barrel as is and was usual in rifles. The Whitworth barrel was hexagonal (six sided) and spiraled down making one turn in twenty inches. The cartridges with the bullet and powder enclosed in paper or linen wrappers varied from at least 3.84 to 4.50 inches long depending on the manufacturer. This was considered to be the most accurate rifle in the world in the 1860's.[11]

---

[11] Dean S. Thomas, *Round Ball to Rimfire: A History of Civil War Small Arms Ammunition* Volume IV (Gettysburg, Pennsylvania: Thomas Publications, 2010), p. 244. John A. Morrow, *The Confederate Whitworth Sharpshooters* (2nd ed.; Atlanta, Georgia: Published by the author, 2002), pp. 9, 17.

# 5

## THE JUNCTION ABANDONED

With the wagons and artillery through the junction of the Lenoir and Kingston Roads, Burnside was ready to begin the next stage of his retreat to the safety of Knoxville's fortifications. Humphrey's badly battered brigade was the first to move. This brigade was so heavily engaged that they were again required to charge the Confederates and drive them back before they could withdraw. In his report of the fighting, Colonel William Humphrey said

> The enemy made a strong effort to get around my left, and at one time had nearly succeeded. He had thrown back the Seventeenth (Michigan) in considerable confusion, and was crowding on as if sure of accomplishing his object. To defeat his move I rode to the Seventeenth and ordered the regiment to charge at once, at the same time ordering the skirmishers from the Twentieth and Second Michigan to be thrown forward, with a yell, to aid the Seventeenth. The charge was finely made, driving the enemy through the woods into the field beyond and throwing his front line into considerable confusion. Before making this move on the enemy I had received orders to withdraw my line.[1]

The charge worked, the Southerners fell back, and Humphrey's Brigade 'fell back unmolested to the position ordered'.

---

[1] *The War of Rebellion*, Series 1, Volume 31, Part 1, pp. 363; Byron Cutcheon, *The Story of the Twentieth Michigan Infantry, July 15th, 1862 to May 30th, 1865* (Lansing, MI: Robert Smith Printing Company, 1904), p. 75.

Humphrey's new position was on the extreme right (north of the Kingston Road) of Chapin's Brigade line of battle which had formed to the west of the William Nelson home. Humphrey's brigade would hold this position until about 1.30 pm when they were relieved by Christ's Brigade. Afterwards, Humphrey's men would go to the rear of the artillery and into a ravine as a reserve and finally out the heat of battle.[2] [See Map 4.]

The next troops to withdraw from this line west of the road junction were the brigades of Siegfried and Schall of Hartranft's Division north of the Kingston Road. They disengaged without difficulty and moved past the Campbell Home and filed off south of the Kingston Road with their right adjoining Colonel Marshall V. Chapin's Brigade of the 23rd Corps. This is the same line of battle as Humphrey's Brigade. The 8th Michigan Cavalry who was stationed on Hartranft's right flank moved back to help protect the artillery on the plateau on the far eastern end of the battlefield.[3]

This left Morrison's Brigade stretched between the Lenoir and Kingston Roads with advancing Confederates on both roads. Earlier Morrison had found 'a good rail fence he determined' that behind it he would 'make a stand and fight the enemy'. This fence as one participant said 'afforded us a slight protection'. They fought the Confederates for about thirty minutes when they were fired on from the rear. Hartranft's Brigades had been withdrawn without Morrison's knowledge, and McLaws' Southerners had advanced past Morrison's line on the Kingston Road. The Thirty-sixth Massachusetts and the Eighth Michigan Infantry were rushed to the fence on the Kingston Road and delivered a volley that temporarily drove the Southerners in their rear away, but more and more Confederates had moved to surround and capture this lone band of men. In his report Morrison stated that at this time he finally received orders to retire. A member of the Thirty-sixth Massachusetts believed that Morrison took it on his own to withdraw from the position between the roads.

---

[2] *The War of Rebellion*, Series 1, Volume 31, Part 1, pp. 363; Byron Cutcheon, *The Story of the Twentieth Michigan Infantry, July 15th, 1862 to May 30th, 1865*, p. 75.
[3] *The War of Rebellion*, Series 1, Volume 31, Part 1, p. 333; Wells, *Autobiography of Samuel Wells*, p. 8.

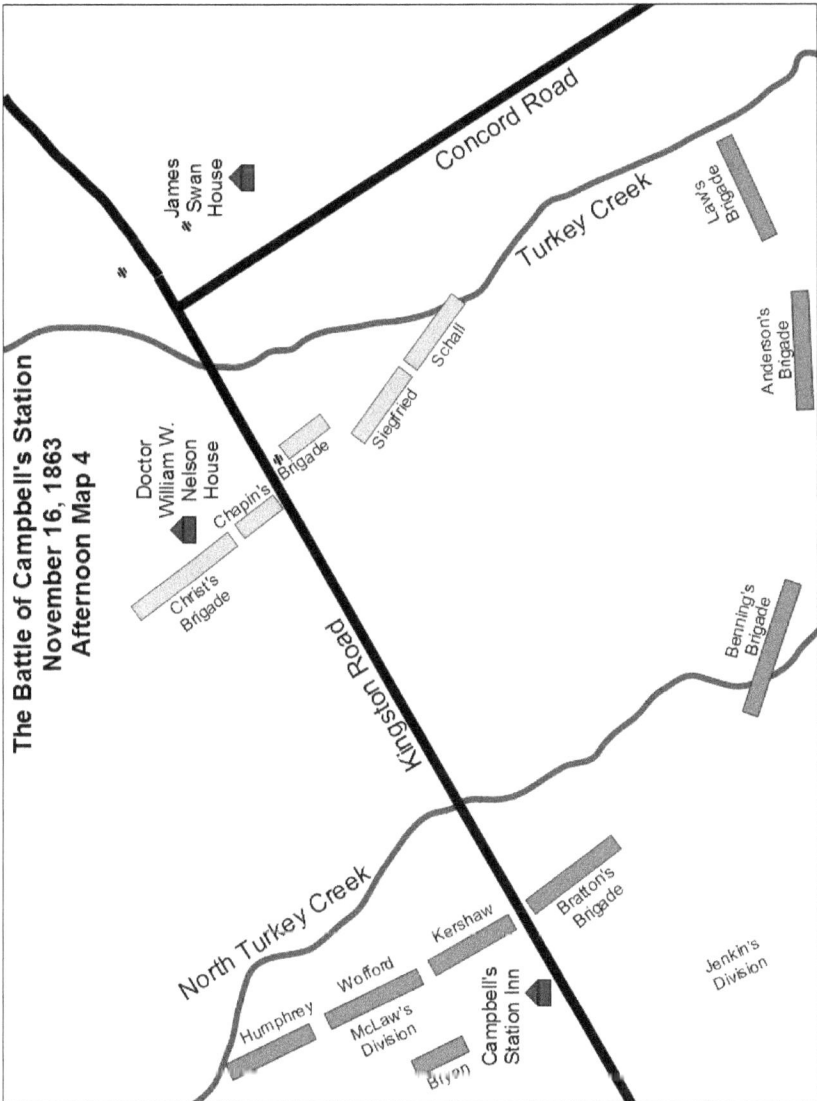

Figure 11
*Map 4 – Battle of Campbell's Station, Early Afternoon*
Created by Christopher L. Augustus

Morrison's Brigade retreated to the Kingston Road and 'double quicked' their pace. The Southerners nearly outflanked the retreating Federals and forced Morrison's men to leave and move north of the road past the Campbell home and through the new line of battle that just formed west of the Nelson Home. They continued until they came to the vicinity of the Concord Road where they were allowed to stop and rest behind the new battle line and support the artillery.[4] [See Map 4.]

---

[4] Henry S. Burrage, *History of the Thirty-Sixth Regiment Massachusetts Volunteers, 1862-1865* (Boston MA: Press of Rockwell and Churchill, 1884), pp. 96-98; John H. Miller, *My War Experiences* (Gardner, MA: Meads Print Co., Gardner, 1912), p. 31; *The War of Rebellion*, Series 1, Volume 31, Part 1, p. 356.

# 6

## '… Like a Mighty Game of Chess …': The Early Moves

The next phase of the fighting took place in a shallow valley about two miles long east to west and about a mile wide north to south. The northern rim is now occupied by Farragut High School, but in 1863 this area was wooded. The eastern rim was less defined, but the most important feature was the small plateau which was traversed on the northern edge by the Kingston Road and the Concord Road immediately to the west. To the south was another low ridge with the Concord Road passing through the eastern end. The western edge was pretty much the route of present day North and South Campbell's Station Roads which did not exist in 1863. The building of the Farragut Town Hall has eliminated much of this elevation. The Kingston Road ran east-west through and at about the center of this valley. [See Map 4.]

There is little evidence left of the battle up to this point. All of the land has been developed. In this part of the battle, however, two of the homes that were there in 1863 are still standing. The brick Campbell's Station Inn is located at the northwestern corner of Campbell's Station Road and Kingston Pike, which was the western end of the valley. This home had been built in circa 1810 by David Campbell, a revolutionary soldier who had earlier acquired the 500 acres for his service in the American Revolution. Campbell sold this property and moved to Middle Tennessee in the early 1800s. After changing hands several times, Mathew Russell purchased the farm in 1858. He and his family were living there during the ensuing fight. During the fighting on the 16th of November 1863, the Russell family and their white horse hid in the basement of the home.

Figure 12
*The Campbell's Station Home*
From the Farragut Folklife Museum Collections

The Dr. William W. Nelson brick home is on the northern side and faces Kingston Pike. As of 2013, this home is located behind the Taco Bell Restaurant. Located about in the middle of the valley, this beautiful two-story brick house had been built circa 1835 for John Campbell, son of David Campbell, by Luke Lea. After changing hands several times, Dr. William Nelson had purchased the property in 1859. Just prior to the arrival of Burnside's army, Eliza Jane Nelson left their home with the family silver and all the women and children both black and white. Mrs. Nelson and others crossed over the ridge behind her home to safety. The Nelson home is often referred to as the Russell house, since Dr. Nelson's granddaughter Julia married Matthew Russell, and the Russell family lived there from the late 1800s for nearly a hundred years.

Figure 13
*The Dr. William W. Nelson Home*
From the Farragut Folklife Museum Collections

The log home of the James Swan family was the third house mentioned in accounts of the battle and has been gone for over a century. It was on the eastern rim of the valley located on a plateau. Some of the Union artillery was placed in the family's orchard.[1]

As the brigades of Humphrey, Morrison, Siegfried, and Schall fought the Confederates west of the Lenoir-Kingston Road junction, Burnside had created a new defensive line across the valley just to the west of the Nelson Home. At first, the line was created by moving some of the brigades to this position and not stopping near the junction. As the brigades were withdrawn from west of the

---

[1] Malcolm L. Shell, *From Frontier Fort to Town Hall: A Brief history of Farragut, Tennessee 1787-2005* (Farragut, TN: Farragut Folklife Museum, 2005), p. 12; Margaret Angel, *Not So Long Ago in the Concord-Farragut Area*, (Nashville, TN: Williams Printing Company, 1986), pp. 59-61.

Campbell's Station Inn, they were placed in line or behind the line of battle to support the artillery.

In the center of this new line was the Second Brigade of the 23rd Corps under the command of Colonel Marshall W. Chapin. Although this was the only brigade from the 23rd Corps present, Brigadier General Julius White, commander of the Second Division of that Corps, was with Chapin's Brigade. The rest of the White's Division had left Lenoirs by train, and to his credit White chose to accompany the men who were in harm's way.

Chapin's line of battle began to the north of the Kingston Road with the 23rd Michigan Infantry which was in front (west) of Dr. Nelson's barn. Next in line was the 13th Kentucky which crossed the Kingston Road. Henshaw's Illinois and the 24th Indiana Artillery Batteries were located in an orchard on a small rise south of the road. The 111th Ohio was next in line and the 107th Illinois the furthest south of the brigade. Due to the configuration of the land, these last two regiments were about 150 yards back from the other two regiments and artillery. Under the command of Captain Uriah M. Laurence, Companies K, F, and B of the 107th Illinois were ordered in front of Henshaw's Battery to help protect guns.

Henshaw's Battery, under the command of Captain Edward C. Henshaw, was armed with two 3.8 inch James rifled cannons and four 6 pounder brass cannons. The 24th Indiana Artillery, under the command of Captain Joseph A. Sims, was armed with six 3.8 James rifled cannons.[2]

After the retreat from the junction, the remnants of Colonel William Humphrey's Brigade were ordered to the right of Chapin's Brigade. The 17th Michigan was to the right of 23rd Corps with the 2nd Michigan and the 20th Michigan Infantry on the extreme right flank. About one o'clock, Colonel Benjamin C. Christ was ordered to send the 29th Massachusetts to assist Humphrey and took a position to the right of Humphrey's depleted regiments. About half an hour later, Humphrey's men were ordered back out of line into a 'shallow ravine'. The rest of Christ's Brigade consisting of the 27th Michigan, 46th New York, and 50th Pennsylvania Infantries were sent forward

---

[2] *The War of Rebellion*, Series 1, Volume 31, Part 1, pp. 315, 379, 384, 386, 389, 391-92; Elijah L. Halstead, Charles L. and Mary L. Childs (eds.), *Green Corn, Fresh Beef and Sick Flour, The Civil War Diary of Corporal Elijah L. Halstead* (Independence, MO: Blue & Grey Book Shoppe, 1999), p. 22.

to replace Humphrey's men. Humphrey's Brigade was to help support the artillery on the hill behind them. At about 3.00 pm Humphrey's Brigade was moved again to the rear of the artillery on the hill. The 29th Massachusetts was on the extreme right of Burnside's infantry. They were about fifty yards from the edge of the woods which were rather open and easily moved through by infantry.[3]

When Hartranft's Division, consisting of Colonel Siegfried and Lt. Colonel Schall's Brigades, left the junction, they came to the new battle line and filed off to the south to connect with Chapin's Brigade in the middle. Thus, a new battle line was formed in the middle of the valley with reserves in their rear near the Concord Road. This line was also supported with artillery in their rear.

Before the Confederates attacked, this artillery in the rear of the battle line consisted of five units and twenty-one cannons. Battery E, 2nd U. S. Artillery under the command of 1st Lieutenant Samuel N. Benjamin with four 20 Pounder Rifles was positioned adjacent to and just north of the Kingston Road. To the right of Benjamin's guns were Batteries L and M consolidated, 3rd U. S. Artillery commanded by 1st Lieutenant Erskine Gittings with four 20 Pounder Parrott Rifles. Behind these two units were the 15th Indiana Artillery under the command of Captain John C. H. Sehlen with three 3 inch Ordnance Rifles and Company D, 1st Rhode Island Artillery under the command of Captain William W. Buckley with six 12 Pounder 'Napoleon' smoothbore. On the south side of the road on the plateau was located the 34th New York Artillery under the command of Captain Jacob Roemer with four 3 inch Rifles. In the ensuing fighting, which began around noon, the two United States artillery batteries would be moved onto the plateau on the south side of the Kingston Road to join the New York Battery.[4]

The 1st Rhode Island had a pleasant surprise when they arrived at their new position. When there was enough light, the battery discovered that during the night one of their 12 Pounder cannons was missing. The company was sure that it had gotten bogged down in the mire and had been captured. As the Rhode Islanders arrived on

---

[3] *The War of Rebellion*, Series 1, Volume 31, Part 1, pp. 358, 362-63; William H. Osborne, *The History of the Twenty-ninth Regiment of Massachusetts Volunteer Infantry in the Late War of the Rebellion* (Boston, MA: Albert J. Wright, Printer, 1877), p. 264.

[4] *The War of Rebellion*, Series 1, Volume 31, Part 1, pp. 315, 333.

the hill at the east end of the Campbell's Station valley, they found the cannon, limber, caisson, and men waiting for them. Sergeant Charles C. Gray was in charge of the supposed lost artillery piece and in the night with good, strong horses had been able to push ahead and bypassed the rest of the battery in the dark.[5]

The Federals did not have to wait long to test the effectiveness of their new position. The Confederate forces of General McLaws, which had advanced on the Kingston Road, were joined with General Jenkins men from the Lenoir Road. For the first time that day the two divisions of Longstreet's Corps were reunited. Due to the delaying tactics of Burnside at the junction, most of the Confederate infantry had had time to catch up with the leading units.

When General McLaws learned that General Longstreet, who had accompanied Jenkins' Division, was 'but 100 or 200 yards' to his right, he reported to Longstreet for further orders. Longstreet ordered Mclaws to deploy his men to the north of the road, 'but not to show it beyond the woods'. When McLaws positioned his line of battle, Brigadier General Joseph B. Kershaw's South Carolina Brigade was on the right nearest the road. Next was Wofford's Georgia Brigade, led that day by Colonel Solon Z. Ruff. Brigadier General Benjamin G. Humphrey's Mississippi Brigade was on the extreme left or northern wing of the division. Brigadier General Goode Bryan's Georgia Brigade was behind the line as a reserve.[6]

Jenkins' brigades were ordered to file off to the south of the Kingston Road into line of battle. Colonel John Bratton's South Carolina Brigade was nearest the Kingston Road. To their right was Brigadier General George T. Anderson's Georgia Brigade, and on the extreme flank was Brigadier General Evander M. Law's Alabama Brigade. Brigadier General Henry L. Benning's Georgia Brigade was in reserve behind the line of battle. General Jerome B. Robertson's Brigade had been left at Lenoirs and Loudon to protect the line of communications with Chattanooga. Jenkins' Division was also unobserved by the Union troops due the wooded nature of the area. This Confederate line was probably about where modern

---

[5] George C. Sumner, *Battery D, First Rhode Island Artillery in the Civil War, 1861-1865* (Providence, RI: Rhode Island Printing Company, 1897), p. 92.

[6] *The War of Rebellion*, Series 1, Volume 31, Part 1, pp. 482-83; Dickert, *History of Kershaw's Brigade*, p. 301.

North and South Campbell's Station Roads are located today.[7] [See Map 4.]

Around noon after the troops were in position, the Confederates moved out of the woods toward the Federal lines drawn up in the middle of the Campbell's Station valley. When the Confederates first came out of the woods, they were mistaken by Burnside's troops for United States troops. Some Union soldiers and newspaper reporters accused the Confederates of wearing United States uniforms. The reason for this confusion was the color of the Richmond Depot uniforms that Longstreet's men were wearing. Longstreet's First Corps had been issued these uniforms after the retreat from Gettysburg in July and their movement to North Georgia in September. These new uniforms had jackets that were made of English imported dark blue-gray material similar to the color of many higher ranking Confederate officers' coats. The close fitting jacket, 'with light blue trousers, which make a line of Confederates resemble that of the enemy, the only difference being the "cut" of the garments – the Federals wearing a loose blouse instead of a tight fitting jacket'.[8]

Sergeant Gray of the 1st Rhode Island Artillery was so sure that the men coming down the hill were Confederates that he fired on them with his carbine. A mounted officer nearby 'severely reprimanded' him for shooting fellow Federal soldiers. Very shortly after the reprimand, the supposed fellow Federals killed the officer's horse in an attempt to kill the officer.[9]

As the Southern lines moved toward their foes, they were unsupported by artillery. The Confederate artillery was still trying to move through the quagmire of mud. The road was in even worse condition than when the Union Artillery had earlier moved over the same roads. Confederate General Jenkins found an unnamed artillery battery and placed them in the edge of the woods while posi-

---

[7] *The War of Rebellion*, Series 1, Volume 31, Part 1, p. 526; Harold B. Simpson, *Hood's Texas Brigade: Lee's Grenadier Guard* (Fort Worth, TX: Landmark Publishing, Inc., 1999), p. 351.

[8] Dickert, *History of Kershaw's Brigade*, p. 268; Thomas M. Arliskas, *Cadet Gray and Butternut Brown: Notes on Confederate Uniforms* (Gettysburg, PA: Thomas Publications, 2006), p. 68; *The War of Rebellion*, Series 1, Volume 31, Part 1, p. 379; Robertson, *Michigan in the War*, p. 431; Bush and Bush, *Black Power to Black Gold*, p. 42.

[9] Sumner, *Battery D, First Rhode Island Artillery in the Civil War, 1861-1865*, p. 92.

tioning Bratton's Brigade. Jenkins left to show Anderson's Brigade where to line up, and Colonel E. Porter Alexander, Chief of Artillery for Longstreet's Corps, moved the artillery back into the woods. With the large amount of Union artillery facing them, Alexander felt that the lone battery would be destroyed.[10]

The Confederates first came down the hill and onto the level ground without firing. With the exception of the one artillerymen, the Federal troops did not fire because of the confusion about what uniform the men wore. There was a ravine (probably present day North Fork of Turkey Creek) that the Southerners moved down into and as they came out began to fire their rifle muskets, and, of course, the fire was quickly returned. At this point the 24th Indiana and Henderson's Illinois Battery also went into action. The artillery on the hill at the eastern end of the valley also began to fire shell and spherical case into the Confederates as they advanced. Three times the Southerners charged out of the woods in the center of the valley along the Kingston Road, and three times they were driven back.[11]

Finally, Longstreet's artillery arrived and was able to support the infantry. Colonel E. Porter Alexander was ordered by Longstreet to place batteries on the south side of the Kingston Road in support of Jenkins' Division. Alexander began firing slowly and increased his firing as the afternoon lengthened.[12]

One of Major Austin Leyden's Georgia Batteries passed Captain William Parker's Virginia Battery to the crest of the hill and beyond. Some of Parker's artillerymen tried to tell the commander of the battery the position was too dangerous, but he did not listen. Before one cannon could be unhooked from the limber, a Union shell hit the limber full of ammunition, exploded the limber, and killed and wounded many of the gun crew.[13]

---

[10] *The War of Rebellion*, Series 1, Volume 31, Part 1, p. 526.

[11] Moore (ed.), *The Rebellion Record*, p. 272; Ezra K. Parker, 'Campaign of Battery D, First Rhode Island Light Artillery, in Kentucky and East Tennessee', *Military Order of the Loyal Legion of the United States*, Volume 41 (Wilmington, NC: Broadfoot Publishing Company, 1993), pp. 274-80; Halstead, *Green Corn, Fresh Beef and Sick Flour, The Civil War Diary of Corporal Elijah L. Halstead*, pp. 23-24; Bush and Bush, *Black Power to Black Gold*, p. 42.

[12] Alexander, *Fighting for the Confederacy*, p. 316.

[13] William M. Evans, 'The Artillery at Knoxville', *Confederate Veteran Magazine*, Volume XXXI (Wilmington, NC: Broadfoot Publishing Company, 1988), p. 424.

The 24th Indiana and Henderson's Illinois batteries supporting the 23rd Corps infantry in the middle of the valley came under extremely heavy fire. The Confederates were armed with 20 Pounder guns which had a longer range and were more accurate than the smaller cannons of these two Union batteries. Also the Federals were down in a valley, and the Confederate artillery was up on a hill, which made it difficult to return fire.

The 24th Indiana had one man wounded and six horses killed, had used up most of their ammunition, and had two of their James Rifles disabled. Henderson's Battery was almost out of ammunition and had two men and eight horses killed. After about twenty minutes of Confederate artillery punishment, the two batteries were ordered by General White to retire to the rear of the rest of the artillery beyond the Concord Road. The two disabled pieces were so badly damaged that the Hoosiers were unable to bring them off the field. Henshaw's Battery had fired a total of six canisters and 252 shells.[14]

Evidently, Colonel John Bratton's South Carolina Brigade, which was directly in front of the 24th Indiana and Henderson's Illinois batteries, paid the price for their bravery. Seventy-one per cent of the casualties in Jenkins' Division were from this one brigade.[15]

With the Confederates infantry withdrawal back into the woods from the center of the field, the Confederate and Union artillery began very heavy firing. The Confederates were plagued with faulty fuses that burned too quickly, too long, or not at all. This resulted in shells and case shot exploding too soon, too late, or not at all. Additionally, many of the rifled cannon projectiles tumbled. A soldier from Bratton's Brigade wrote that they 'were forced to endure the terror of bursting shell from both sides, a very severe duel going on; the shell from (their) own guns doing more harm than that of the enemy'. A member of the 15th Indiana Artillery described the Confederate fire as, 'Their ammunition was poor and only created a noise, as so much blank ammunition would have done'.[16]

---

[14] *The War of Rebellion*, Series 1, Volume 31, Part 1, p. 392; Halstead, *Green Corn, Fresh Beef and Sick Flour, The Civil War Diary of Corporal Elijah L. Halstead*, pp. 23-24; Bush and Bush, *Black Power to Black Gold*, p. 42.

[15] *The War of Rebellion*, Series 1, Volume 31, Part 1, p. 526.

[16] *The War of Rebellion*, Series 1, Volume 31, Part 1, p. 478; James Lide Coker, *History of Company G, Ninth S.C. Regiment, Infantry, S.C. Army and of Company E,*

James H. Miller of the 36th Massachusetts was part of Colonel Morrison's Brigade and had been sent to the rear of Burnside's forces near the Concord Road. The Massachusetts troops were resting in what they thought was a safe place. Miller and some of his company were sitting on a pile of fence rails when he 'saw what looked to be a black spot coming right toward where [they] sat. [He] sung out to move quick and the next instant the piece of iron struck the pile of rails in good shape!' The Confederate shell's fuse did work that time.[17]

Private William J. Joiner, an artilleryman in one of Major Austin Leyden's 9th Georgia Battalion, was 'kneeling behind a limber on his right knee, facing to the right & putting a fuze in a shell placed on the ground & using both hands'. A 20 Pounder

> shot struck one of the wheel horses in the chest, ranged through the length of his body a little downward, wrecked the splinter bar of the limber, & passed just under the axle & struck this poor fellow's left leg above the knee, his left arm above the elbow & his right arm at or below it leaving all three only hanging by shreds.

Joiner 'was still alive when carried off the field on a stretcher, but died from loss of blood soon after'.[18]

Confederate General Longstreet and his staff were near Captain Pichegru Woolfolk's Virginia Battery during some of the heavy firing. One of Woolfolk's 20 Pounder Parrott cannons exploded when fired. Whether this was caused by a premature fuse ignition or faulty casting of the cannon by the Tredegar Iron Works in Richmond, Virginia, is unknown. Pieces of the cannon flew in all directions, but, fortunately, no one including General Longstreet was injured. This was Longstreet's second close call of the day. Longstreet's luck finally ran out on 6 May 1864 when he was accidentally

---

*Sixth S.C. Regiment, Infantry, S.C. Army* (Greenwood, SC: The Attic Press, Inc., 1979 reprint of the original), p. 141; Fredrick W. Fout, *The Dark Days of the Civil War, 1861 to 1865* (Lexington, KY: Forgotten Books, 2012, a reprint of the original 1904 edition), p. 210.

[17] Miller, *My War Experiences*, p. 31.

[18] Alexander, *Fighting for the Confederacy*, p. 316; Hess, Earl J., *The Knoxville Campaign: Burnside and Longstreet in East Tennessee* (Knoxville, TN: The University of Tennessee Press, 2012), p. 67.

fired on by his own men. He was hit in the throat and right arm, which left him with permanent disabilities the rest of his life.[19]

Sometime during the artillery duel, a rabbit came running through Parker's Virginia Battery. One of the young artillerymen yelled above the roar of cannon, 'Go it, old hare, I'd run too if I didn't have a reputation to sustain!' The firing was stopped for a short time so that some unidentified women and children could flee the line of fire. Parker was ordered to move his four 3 inch Ordnance Rifles to five different positions during the fight. One of these moves almost ended in disaster when Kershaw's Confederate Brigade mistook the battery for the enemy and was about to open fire when the mistake was discovered.[20]

Exploding shells and bullets were not the only danger that day. Battery D, 1st Rhode Island which was shorthanded had acquired several infantrymen to help with the mules pulling two of their limbers. Usually horses, which were trained to remain quiet during firing and exploding shells, were used to pull the limbers, but not enough horses were available. While in the position of firing, 1st Lieutenant Ezar K. Parker heard very loud profanity to his rear. Turning around, he found two mule teams charging each other in fright, 'and when they met they began to climb up each other … After getting up in the air a good distance, the leading pairs of each team fell over. Underneath each was thrown a man.' When a lull came in the battle the 'cannoneers went to the assistance of the mule guards. One man was severely bruised, though no bones were broken.' The mules were moved further back from the firing line and finally settled down.[21]

While the battle was raging, General Burnside sent a telegraph operator with several soldiers to Concord where the telegraph wires were located. Burnside needed to get an important message to Colonel William P. Sanders near Knoxville. The message was an

---

[19] Alexander, *Fighting for the Confederacy*, p. 316; Hess, Earl J., *The Knoxville Campaign: Burnside and Longstreet in East Tennessee* (Knoxville, TN: The University of Tennessee Press, 2012), p. 67; Hewett, *Supplement to the Official Records of the Union and Confederate Armies*, Series 5, p. 685.

[20] Robert K. Krick, *Parker's Virginia Battery C.S.A.* (Berryville, VA: Virginia Book Company, 1975), pp. 205-206.

[21] Parker, 'Campaign of Battery D, First Rhode Island Light Artillery, in Kentucky and East Tennessee', pp. 277-78.

order for Sanders to form a line of battle on the Kingston Road near Knoxville to protect his retreating army and slow up the advancing Confederates. After several attempts this plan was given up due to the fact that the Confederates occupied Concord in force. Burnside asked the commander of his escort, Lieutenant Thomas E. Milchrist of the Company G, 112th Illinois Mounted Infantry, to seek a volunteer to deliver the message to Knoxville. Private John Crow immediately volunteered and successfully reached Knoxville after a dangerous ride. During the siege of Knoxville, Burnside sent for Crow, who did not receive the message. When Burnside left East Tennessee, he left a letter for Crow thanking him for his perilous ride and fifty dollars 'as a personal gift from himself in reward for his brave conduct'.[22]

Some of the Confederate forces in Concord belonged to Hart's Cavalry Brigade and had been sent behind the Confederate lines to capture the town and any enemy soldiers found. No Union soldiers were found, but they 'found what was far more important' to the always hungry Confederates than 'a batch of prisoners'. Concord had been the location of a Federal army bakery where the Confederates found a 'batch of fresh-baked dough – 2,000 loaves of good wheat bread – something (the Confederates) had not seen or tasted for a month or more, probably more, as (their) wagons could not keep up with (their) rapid moves, and more often than not (they) were dividing rations with (their) horses'.[23]

---

[22] Thompson, *History of the 112th Regiment of Illinois Volunteer Infantry in the Great War of the Rebellion 1862-1865*, pp. 135-36; *The War of Rebellion*, Series 1, Volume 31, Part 1, p. 275.

[23] Minnich, *The Cavalry at Knoxville*, pp. 11-12.

# 7

## '... LIKE A MIGHTY GAME OF CHESS ...': THE LATER MOVES

After Longstreet's three unsuccessful attempts to break through the center of the Union lines, he developed a new plan. McLaws' Division, north of the Kingston Road, was ordered to move forward and engage the enemy. One of McLaws' infantry brigades and some of Hart's Cavalry were to be sent around to the left of the line and attack the Federals' right flank. Longstreet also ordered Jenkins to send two brigades around to the right to crush the Union's left flank. Both of these attacks were to occur simultaneously.[1]

General McLaws immediately began to place his brigades for the movement forward. Beginning on the north side of the Kingston Road, he placed General Kershaw's South Carolina brigade. Next in line was Wofford's Georgians with Bryan's Georgia Brigade behind these two brigades as a second line. Humphrey's Mississippi Brigade accompanied by some of Hart's Cavalry were on the extreme left of McLaws' Division in the hilly woods. After waiting for the attack on the right to begin, McLaws ordered his division to advance without hearing or seeing the attack on Jenkins' flank. General Longstreet rode over and halted McLaws' advance to wait for Jenkins' attack.[2]

Humphrey's Mississippians evidently did not receive the latest order and continued forward, when the rest of the division stopped. The Mississippians eventfully ran into the 29th Massachusetts Infan-

---

[1] *The War of Rebellion*, Series 1, Volume 31, Part 1, p. 458; Longstreet, *From Manassas to Appomattox*, p. 493.
[2] *The War of Rebellion*, Series 1, Volume 31, Part 1, p. 483.

try. Colonel Ebenezer W. Pierce of the 29th and Colonel Benjamin C. Christ commanding the brigade had feared that the Confederates would try to flank the 29th Massachusetts which was the extreme right regiment in Burnside's Army. Colonel Pierce sent Companies A and I into the woods where they found the Mississippians 'approaching stealthily from tree to tree' in an attempt to surprise the Federals. Skirmishing continued for some time between the two sides, until the numerically superior Confederates began to out flank the Federal skirmishers.

When Colonel Christ was apprised of the situation, he ordered the skirmishers to rejoin their regiment and his whole brigade to retreat. As they moved back, they changed fronts and faced west to northwest toward the woods. As this movement took place, the Confederates emerged from the woods behind what had been the Christ's Brigade front. The Confederates were held in check with the support of Battery D, 1st Rhode Island Light Artillery which fired twenty-five or thirty rounds into the Southerners. Christ's Brigade moved to a new position beyond the creek (now named Turkey Creek) and onto the hill behind. As the 29th Massachusetts formed their new position, Generals Burnside and Ferrero applauded the successful withdrawal.[3]

After the Confederates were repulsed on the Union's right flank, General Potter, the 9th Corps commander, was ordered by Burnside to have mounted men go beyond both flanks to determine if the enemy was there. Potter sent one of his aides, Captain Clifford Coddington, with two companies of mounted men to the right. They crossed the ridge on the right flank into the next valley where they found no sign of the Confederates. When Coddington made his report, Potter ordered the mounted companies to reoccupy the woods on Christ's new right flank. Potter sent Captain Augustus A. Dunn with Companies D and F of the 112 Illinois Mounted Infantry to move toward Concord. Dunn found the Southerners between Campbell's Station and Concord. These two companies remained in

---

[3] Osborne, *The History of the Twenty-ninth Regiment of Massachusetts Volunteer Infantry in the Late War of the Rebellion*, pp. 264-65; Parker, 'Campaign of Battery D, First Rhode Island Light Artillery, in Kentucky and East Tennessee', pp. 276-77.

the woods, skirmished with the southern cavalry, and sent reports to General Potter.[4]

Meanwhile, on the south side of the Kingston Road, Confederate General Jenkins was under the impression that McLaws was supposed to attack first and waited for the sounds of battle on McLaws' front. At about three o'clock Jenkins began to position his men for the attack. Bratton's Brigade of South Carolinians were to remain in position with their left on the road. Benning's 'small' Brigade of Georgians were held in reserve. Anderson's Georgians were somewhat detached to the right and were next in line opposite the enemy cannon. Law's Alabamians were to move out further to their right, ascend the hill to their south, and then move eastward until they were on or behind Union General Hartranft's left flank. General Longstreet remained near Law's and Anderson's Brigades for a short time to assure that his orders were carried out. Fearful of attracting Union fire, he rode back alone to reach the rest of Jenkins' Division.[5]

Jenkins' official report stated,

> The hills and ground over which (Law's) column was required to pass was very difficult, being covered with a close undergrowth of scraggy oaks, and the distance having been increased by the enemy's front lines going back under fire of our artillery, it required considerable time to attain the desired position upon their flank, their lines having open ground to retire upon, being able to move at least as rapidly as (Law's) column.[6]

When Law finally reported that he was in position, Jenkins ordered Anderson's Brigade to move forward and attack. When Jenkins rode forward to find Law's Brigade, he discovered that Law had not gone far enough and sent word to Anderson's Brigade to halt and await further orders. Law was then ordered 'to make the attack with his brigade independently of Anderson'.[7] General Law

[4] *The War of Rebellion*, Series 1, Volume 31, Part 1, p. 134; Thompson, *History of the 112th Regiment of Illinois Volunteer Infantry in the Great War of the Rebellion 1862-1865*, p. 134.

[5] *The War of Rebellion*, Series 1, Volume 31, Part 1, p. 526; Longstreet, *From Manassas to Appomattox*, p. 494.

[6] *The War of Rebellion*, Series 1, Volume 31, Part 1, p. 526.

[7] *The War of Rebellion*, Series 1, Volume 31, Part 1, p. 526.

advanced forward only to overlap Anderson's Brigade. The result was that Hartranft's left hand force was able to change fronts and successfully withdraw to a new position on the east side of the Concord Road.

Both Jenkins and Longstreet blamed General Law with losing the chance to destroy Burnside's Federals. In his after action report, Jenkins stated that Law's 'causeless and inexcusable movement lost us the few moments in which success from this point could be attained'. Writing years later, General Law blamed Longstreet for not ordering McLaw's Division to move sooner and thus distract the enemy while he made his flanking movement.[8] [See Excursus 1, 'Feuding Confederate Generals' for background on some of the feuding within the ranks at Campbell's Station.]

Confederate General Law's attack may not have succeeded, even if he had moved faster and further before turning to his left. His movements had been observed by both Generals Burnside and Potter. Roemer's New York Battery lent support to Hartranft's men and helped in the confusion that plagued the Confederate advance. Potter had sent orders to Hartranft to withdraw as Law's and Anderson's troops moved forward.[9]

With these latest flank attacks by the Confederates, General Burnside realized that his defense in the middle of the valley was no longer practical. He began to order troops to fall back to a new position east of the Concord Road intersection. Christ's Brigade to the north of the Kingston Road had already withdrawn past the creek to their rear when the Confederates tried to get behind them. Hartranft's men south of the Kingston Road were ordered to cross the creek and the Concord Road. Hartranft's regiments were able to withdraw with a minimum of difficulty and came into line with Christ's Brigade at the base of the plateau in front of the artillery. So far everything had worked well for the Union troops. Chapin's

[8] J. Gary Laine and Morris M. Penny, *Law's Alabama Brigade in the War Between the Union and the Confederacy* (Shippensburg, PA: White Mane Publishing Co., 1996), p. 205; Longstreet, *From Manassas to Appomattox*, p. 494; *The War of Rebellion*, Series 1, Volume 31, Part 1, pp. 458, 527.
[9] *The War of Rebellion*, Series 1, Volume 31, Part 1, pp. 274, 334; Bolton, *The Civil War Journal of Colonel William J. Bolton, 51st Pennsylvania, April 20, 1861 – August 2, 1865*, p. 150.

Brigade of the 23rd Corps remained in the valley to cover the withdrawal of the 9th Corps brigades.[10] [See Map 5.]

In order to cover the withdrawal, Chapin was forced to stretch his line of skirmishers across the entire front of Burnside's army. He skillfully moved his 'brigade slowly to the rear, occasionally halting and checking the enemy. During this movement the fire from the enemy's artillery and infantry was very heavy, but the movement was performed deliberately and steadily as though the regiments were on drill.' As Chapin's Brigade fell back, the Confederates made a charge on the left flank of the brigade. Chapin ordered the 107th Illinois to change fronts to face this new threat, and the Confederates were 'handsomely repulsed'. Chapin continued to fall 'slowly back until' they came into line at the base of the plateau with Christ's line to the north of the Kingston Road and Hartrantf's line to the south.[11]

Just prior to the retrograde movements of Chapin's men, Major Isaac R. Sherwood commanding the 111th Ohio had a Confederate shell explode 'about two feet from (his) left ear, and knocked (him) down'. After regaining his feet, he received orders to start a retreat to the rear. Remarkably, his only injury was the permanent loss of hearing in his left ear. With Chapin's men in position, Hartranft's Division moved from the foot of the plateau to the top. This would force the Confederates to stretch their lines even further in order to flank Burnside's command.[12]

The movement of the troops in the Campbell's Station Valley could easily be observed by the artillerymen, their infantry support, and Generals Burnside and Potter. 'This retreat over that field was a sight so grand and beautiful in its management that it attracted the attention of every officer and man who could leave his command to witness it.' Oliver C. Bosbyshell of the 48th Pennsylvania Infantry best described the scene of the maneuvers of Federal regiments on an open plain as 'like a mighty game of chess'. Bosbyshell was not the only one to use the analogy of chess in his description of the troop movements.

---

[10] *The War of Rebellion*, Series 1, Volume 31, Part 1, pp. 274, 334, 384.

[11] *The War of Rebellion*, Series 1, Volume 31, Part 1, p. 384.

[12] Sherwood, *Memories of War*, p. 84.

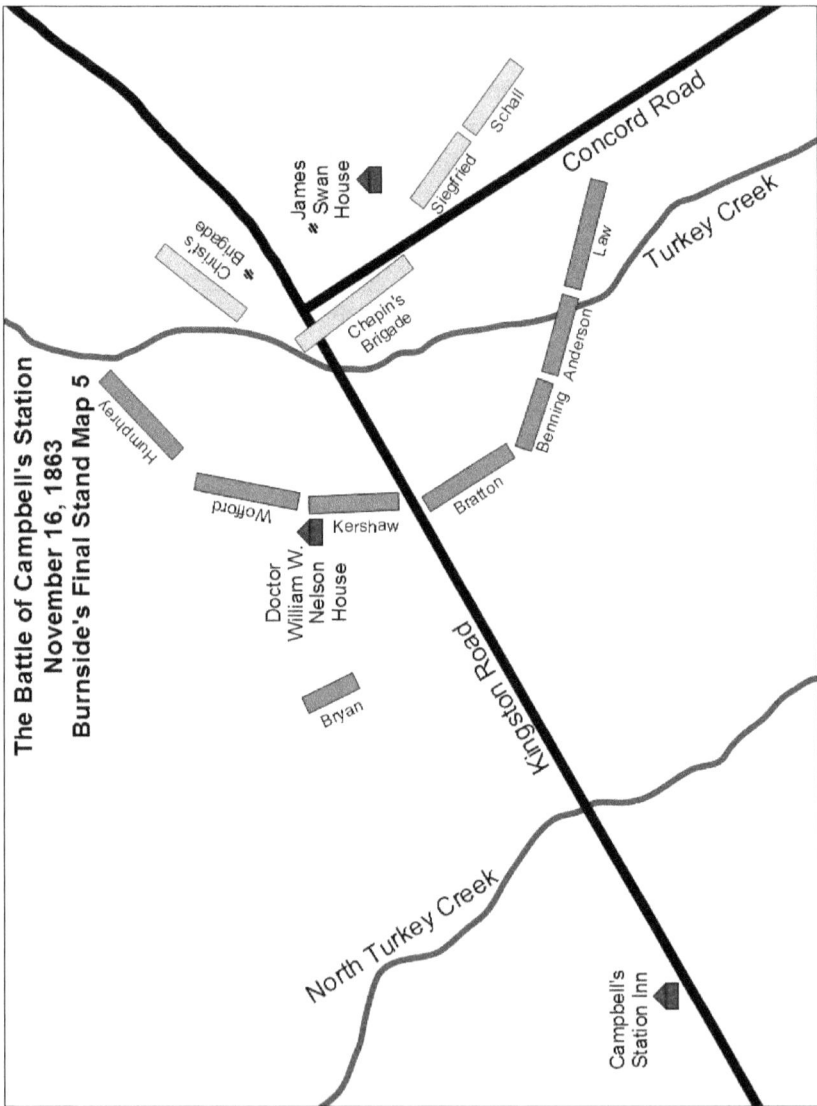

Figure 14
*Map 5 – Burnside's Final Stand.*
Created by Christopher L. Augustus.

A newspaper correspondent wrote,

> Insignificant as the present fight may appear in comparison with others of this war, it certainly will rank among those in which real generalship was displayed. Every motion, every evolution, was made with the precision and regularity of the pieces on a chess board.[13]

With the withdrawal of the Federal troops to the east of the Concord Road, Captain Dunn and his two companies of the 112th Illinois Mounted Infantry were finally forced to give up their position on the that road. When Dunn reported to General Potter on reaching the army's new position, Potter again ordered him out to the left to occupy hills east of the Concord Road. Captain Dunn's orders were to hold this position until he received other orders.[14]

---

[13] Bosbyshell, Oliver C., *The 48th in the War*, p. 132; Moore, *The Rebellion Record*, Volume 7, p. 273; Carruth, *History of the Thirty-Fifth Regiment, Massachusetts, Volunteers* p. 183; James C. Fitzpatrick, 'Dispatches', *The New York Herald*, December 6, 1863, p. 1.

[14] Thompson, *History of the 112th Regiment of Illinois Volunteer Infantry in the Great War of the Rebellion 1862-1865*, p. 134.

## Excursus 4

### The Story of the Lost Sword

An interesting story that took thirty-four years to unfold started at the Battle of Campbell's Station. Lieutenant William H. Hodgkins was adjutant of the 36th Massachusetts Infantry in 1863. He wore a sword that had been presented to him by his Sunday School of the First Congregational Church in Charlestown, Massachusetts. The sword's upper brass scabbard was engraved with his name and who had presented it to him. On 14 September 1863 Hodgkins had been sent to Massachusetts to bring back some drafted men but had left his sword with the regiment marching to East Tennessee. Hodgkins did not return to the regiment until 11 December 1863, after the Battle of Campbell's Station. Orderly Sergeant John W. Fairbank, Company K of the same regiment was promoted to the rank of 2nd Lieutenant while Hodgkins was in Massachusetts. The newly commissioned Fairbank needed a sword in his new position and was allowed to wear Hodgkins's sword until one could be obtained. During the Battle of Campbell's Station, Lieutenant Fairbank was wounded in the leg as the 36th Massachusetts was retreating to the last position of the day. He was helped off the field and recovered, but Hodgkins' sword was left on the battlefield.

Evidently, the sword was picked up by an unidentified South Carolina soldier as they advanced across the field. In 1897, thirty-four years after the battle, the Southerner wrote a letter to the Boston newspaper requesting information about William H. Hodgkins. In the letter he stated that he wanted to return the sword to Hodgkins. Hodgkins soon wrote to South Carolina and was reunited with his lost sword.[15]

---

[15] Henry S. Burrage, 'How I Recovered My Sword', in *Military Order of the Loyal Legion of the United States* Volume 17 (Wilmington, NC: Broadfoot Publishing Company, 1992), pp. 61-62; Bosbyshell, *The 48th in the War*, p. 80.

# 8

## Final Stand

Late in the afternoon, the final battle line of the day was formed by the tired and hungry Union soldiers of the 9th and 23rd Corps. This scene is depicted in Paul J. Long's 1986 painting of 'Battle of Campbell's Station'. The original painting hangs in the lobby of the city of Farragut's Town Hall.

The artist's perspective is from behind the Union lines looking west toward the advancing Confederates. The Kingston Road begins in the lower left corner of the painting. The man on horseback with the domed hat is General Ambrose Burnside, Commander of the Army of the Ohio, and the other horseman is General Robert B. Potter, Commander of the 9th Corps. The Dr. William Nelson house is the closest of the two brick homes, with the Campbell's Station Inn-Russell home on the horizon.

In anticipation of further retreat to Knoxville, all of Buckley's Battery D, 1st Rhode Island Artillery, except one section of two 12 pounder cannon under the command of Ezra K. Parker, was ordered back about one mile at about 4.00 pm. Buckley's four cannon were placed in reserve on the hill where the modern day Lovell Road intersects with the Kingston Road. The 1st Rhode Island waited there in reserve until about 5.30 pm as it was gathering darkness. With no indication that the battery would be needed to repulse the enemy, it was ordered to proceed to Knoxville. Buckley's two

Figure 15
*The Battle of Campbell's Station, by Paul J. Long*
From the Farragut Folklife Museum Collections

sections of artillery had a head start on most of the army and arrived in the city about 10.30 pm that night.[1]

As it became darker, Burnside began to order the two divisions of the 9th Corps infantry and artillery toward Knoxville. The first to retire was the division of General Ferrero followed by General Hartranft's Division. The 34th New York Artillery, a part of Ferrero's Division, had fired 441 shots that day.

Colonel Chapin's Division of the 23rd Corps supported by some mounted men was left holding the entire line across the Kingston Road. In fact, Colonel Chapin was no longer in command of the brigade. He …

> had been unwell for a number of days but had refused to leave the field while the enemy was in front, was now suffering so that he was ordered to quit his post, and the command devolved upon Colonel William E. Hobson, who led the men from the field and conducted the retreat to Knoxville.[2]

As artillery units moved to the rear, there were finally only two artillery units left firing at the Confederates: Battery D, 2nd United States Artillery and the two 12 Pounders of Parker's Battery D, 1st Rhode Island Artillery. 'When it became so dark that one could not see twenty-five yards', Parker's two gun section of artillery was ordered to withdraw. When Parker's men tried to move the mules with the limbers forward to hitch the cannon to them, the mules refused to advance to within a hundred yards of the cannon. Parker finally ordered the men to drag the cannon to where the mules were located and the artillery reached Knoxville by 5.00 am the next morning.[3]

After night had fallen, Battery D, 2nd United States Artillery limbered their cannon and began an all night retreat to Knoxville. The battery's four 20 Pounders 'had fired 429 rounds'. The 2nd Brigade, 2nd Division, 23rd Corps now under the command of Colonel Hob-

[1] *The War of Rebellion*, Series 1, Volume 31, Part 1, p. 336; Parker, 'Campaign of Battery D, First Rhode Island Light Artillery, in Kentucky and East Tennessee', p. 278.

[2] *The War of Rebellion*, Series 1, Volume 31, Part 1, p. 334; Moore, *The Rebellion Record*, Volume 7, p. 273; Roemer, *Reminiscences of the War of the Rebellion, 1861-1865*, p. 164.

[3] Parker, 'Campaign of Battery D, First Rhode Island Light Artillery, in Kentucky and East Tennessee', pp. 278-79.

son left their lines and followed the rest of the Union retreat to Knoxville. Hobson's Brigade was the rearguard of Burnside's army.[4]

Except for the wounded, dead, and dying, the only Union troops known to be left at Campbell's Station were several companies of the 112th Illinois Mounted Infantry. Their duty was to keep hundreds of large fires going to deceive the Confederates into believing that Burnside's army was still camped there.[5]

However, several companies of the 112th Illinois were left in the area. Captain Augustus A. Dunn with companies D and F had earlier in the day been sent out to a hill near the Concord Road by General Potter. Potter had forgotten Dunn's men and the 112th regimental command did not know where they were. Dunn and his men could hear in the darkness the Confederate infantry to their right and to their rear and Southern cavalry to their front. Despite urging from his officers and men, Dunn was determined to follow orders and remain until General Potter relieved them.

Finally, Dunn agreed to allow Lieutenant James G. Armstrong of Company F to send Private Benjamin W. Todd to find General Potter. Of course by this time, General Potter was a long way from Campbell's Station, and Todd could not have found the general. Whether Todd knew this or not, he quickly returned claiming that he had verbal orders for the companies to rejoin the army on its way to Knoxville. By tearing down fences and the darkness hiding them, Dunn's two companies were able to reach the Kingston Road and finally return to their regiment. As Dunn's command left, the Confederate cavalry fired as they retreated, but there were no reported casualties.[6]

Captain Sylvester F. Otman of the 112th Illinois Mounted Infantry had prior to 16 November 1863 been ordered to guard a section of the Holston River (now Tennessee River) to the southeast of Campbell's Station. Otman was at his northern picket post at Lowe's Ferry, located near United States Admiral David G. Farragut's birthplace. On hearing the battle raging at Campbell's Station, Captain Otman took his men and started down the river to

---

[4] *The War of Rebellion*, Series 1, Volume 31, Part 1, pp. 345, 379.

[5] Thompson, *History of the 112th Regiment of Illinois Volunteer Infantry in the Great War of the Rebellion 1862-1865*, p. 134.

[6] Thompson, *History of the 112th Regiment of Illinois Volunteer Infantry in the Great War of the Rebellion 1862-1865*, pp. 134-35.

gather his other pickets. He was able to reach parts of Company E commanded by Sergeant John E. Gharrett. Further down the river were even more members of the Company E under the command of Sergeant Solomon Dixon. Sergeant Dixon and his men had to be left without rescue or warning due to the presents of a large number of Southern cavalry who blocked the way.[7]

Since Sergeant Dixon's post was much further down the river, they were unaware of what was going on around them until a Confederate cavalryman came to the other side of the river looking for a relative in the 112th Illinois. Realizing his relative might be among them, the Southerner tried to warn the Unionist of their imminent capture. Dixon and his men thought it was an attempt to force them to leave their position. Thinking that it was time for his men to be relieved, Sergeant Dixon sent two men to Concord to find out about their replacements. While the two men were gone, the 'relief squad came. It consisted of one hundred men of the 5th Georgia Cavalry.[8] They said (Dixon's men) were wanted in Concord.' Sergeant Dixon and his command became prisoners of war, and many of them would die in Confederate prisons.[9]

At the Campbell's Station battlefield, the Confederates pulled back at nightfall and camped, expecting to finish the fight the next day. One of the Georgia artillerymen who had been injured when their caisson was blown up early in the day was still on the battlefield. The wounded man was making such pitiful moans that Captain Stephen Winthrop, an Englishman on General Alexander's staff, crawled out to him. He discovered the man had the lower part of his face and tongue blown away. Realizing that the man was going to die, and therefore he could not help him recover, Winthrop crawled back and found Captain William M. Parker of Parker's Virginia Battery. Parker had been a physician prior to the war and often treated his fellow soldiers. Winthrop begged for morphine so he

---

[7] Thompson, *History of the 112th Regiment of Illinois Volunteer Infantry in the Great War of the Rebellion 1862-1865*, pp. 136-37; Mary U. Rothrock (ed.), *The French Broad-Holston County: A History of Knox County, Tennessee* (Knoxville, TN: East Tennessee Historical Society, 1946), p. 416.

[8] This is a mistaken identification since the 5th Georgia Cavalry was in South Carolina on this date. Timothy Daiss, *In the Saddle: Exploits of the 5th Georgia Cavalry* (Atglen, PA: Schiffer Publishing, 1999), pp. 15-16.

[9] Thompson, *History of the 112th Regiment of Illinois Volunteer Infantry in the Great War of the Rebellion 1862-1865*, p. 457.

could return and give it to the suffering man to ease his pain. Winthrop, a bachelor, insisted he go alone since he was single, while the married Parker insisted that he go because he was a doctor. In the end, Parker and Winthrop went together and administered the pain killer.[10]

There was little food for the tired and hungry Southerners that night. The plight of the 4th Alabama illustrates the condition of the Confederate troops. All the rations that the regiment had received were potatoes. When they were evenly divided among the officers and men, each man received two. Lieutenants Robert T. Coles and William Turner were so hungry they decided to gamble for the four potatoes between them. Turner won, and Coles had nothing for supper.[11]

The next morning, Tuesday, 17th of November, the Confederates moved forward expecting to renew the fighting of the day before. Instead of battle the Southerners found only the unburied dead, the dying, and the wounded remnants of Burnside's retreating army. At approximately 8.00 am, Longstreet began his pursuit of Burnside's retreating army.

As Longstreet's troops moved into the lines recently occupied by Burnside's army, they met an older woman who lived in a log cabin in a clearing. She was very upset. With all the destruction, pain, and death that resulted from this engagement, one small calamity had happened to her. The Union soldiers in their haste to retreat had upset her ash hopper![12]

Detailed figures on the number of killed, wounded, and missing in Burnside's Army of the Ohio will be found in Appendix B. The 9th and 23rd Corps suffered a total of 31 men killed, 211 wounded, and 96 missing for a total of 338 casualties. Interestingly, the casualties illustrate where the most severe fighting took place, and who did the hardest fighting. Of the six brigades of infantry, numerous

---

[10] William M. Evans, 'The Artillery at Knoxville', *Confederate Veteran Magazine* Volume XXXI (Wilmington, NC: Broadfoot Publishing Company, 1988), p. 424; Krick, *Parker's Virginia Battery C.S.A.*, pp. 206, 346.

[11] Alexander Mendoza, *Confederate Struggle For Command: General James Longstreet and the First Corps in the West* (College Station, TX: Texas A&M University Press, 2008), p. 125.

[12] McLaws, *A Soldier's General*, p. 221; Thompson, *History of the 112th Regiment of Illinois Volunteer Infantry in the Great War of the Rebellion 1862-1865*, p. 458; Evans, Evans, 'The Artillery at Knoxville', p. 424.

batteries, and cavalry units, Colonel William Humphrey's Brigade, which fought up the hill from the creek at the beginning of the battle, suffered 42% of the killed, 53% of the wounded, and 22% of the missing. Humphrey's Brigade accounted for 43% of the total casualties for the whole Union forces engaged at Campbell's Station. The 17th Michigan Infantry of Humphrey's Brigade, who had been left as the rear guard at the beginning of the battle, had 54% of the killed, 46% of the wounded, and 71% of the missing men in Humphrey's Brigade.

Among the dead at Campbell's Station was Lieutenant P. Marion Holmes of Company B, 36th Massachusetts Infantry of Morrison's Brigade. Holmes had been wounded at Blue Springs, northeast of Knoxville on 10 October 1863. Although his 'wound had not fully healed, had made the march from Lenoir's with great difficultly. But he would not leave his men.' The men of his company tried to carry his body with them as they left Campbell's Station but lacked proper transportation. They buried Holmes near the place of his death and clearly marked his grave. Several weeks later, his father came and retrieved his remains; he was buried in his hometown of Charlestown, Massachusetts.[13]

The Confederate losses at Campbell's Station are not as detailed as the Union losses. [See Appendix C.] Only General Jenkins reported his division's losses and only gives the brigade numbers, but not by regiments. Jenkins reported a total of 22 killed, 152 wounded, and none missing for a total of 174 casualties. Again as with the Union losses, the areas of most severe fighting are evident. Confederate Colonel John Bratton's South Carolina Brigade of Jenkins' Division had 82% of the killed, 70% of the wounded, and, therefore, 71% of the casualties of three brigades engaged in the battle. Bratton's Brigade had been the forces primarily engaged with Union Colonel William Humphrey's Brigade at the beginning of the battle. They were also the brigade who had later charged into the 23rd Corps artillery in the middle of the Campbell Station Valley.

One of the strangest deaths on the battlefield occurred as Confederate General Bratton's Brigade charged down the hill into the 23rd Corps in the early afternoon. A Federal shell exploded near the middle of the 5th South Carolina Infantry. One of the casualties was

---

[13] Burrage, 'Burnside's East Tennessee Campaign', pp. 96-97.

Private Robert McKnight whose arm was blown off by a shell fragment. He survived this terrible wound and received a discharge. However, McKnight's severed arm hit Private Lorraine Swann in the head, and splattered blood and brain matter over those around him. Private Swann expired immediately.[14]

No report was found of Confederate Lafayette McLaws' Division losses or any of his brigade commanders. Captain Wyatt R. McClain of the Fifty-first Georgia Infantry in Bryan's Brigade reported that his regiment suffered no casualties.[15] Although one of McLaws' brigades had attempted to turn the Union Army's right flank, they were not as severely engaged in the fighting as Jenkins' Division. McLaws' losses were probably not as high as Jenkins' casualties, but assuming that they were similar to those of Jenkins, their loss would have been about 174. Total Confederate losses were probably about 348.

The fighting if not the war had left the western area of Knox County.

While many historians have passed over the importance of the Battle of Campbell's Station, within weeks a map of the battle appeared on the 7 December 1863 front page of the New York Tribune. An unnamed artist/reporter had drawn a sketch of the battlefield and mailed the article to the newspaper. There another artist redrew the map on a block of wood. This wood block was carved, inked, and then used to print the map that appeared in the newspaper. Due to such factors as speed, crudeness of the wooden block media, size constraints, and other factors, newspaper images during the War were usually simplified and often distorted from the original drawings. All of these factors may have influenced the finished product that appeared in the newspaper.

There are some interesting and odd features on this map. The Lenoir Road appears to be the main road, and the Kingston Road appears to be a secondary road. The Concord Road was not included. Most maps place north at the top of map; on this map west is at the top.

---

[14] Mendoza, *Confederate Struggle For Command*, p. 125.

[15] Wyatt R. McClain, 'Report of Captain Wyatt R. McClain, Fifty-first Georgia Infantry Volunteers, C.S. Army on the engagement at Campbell's Station, November 16, 1863', *Supplement to the Official Records of the Union and Confederate Armies*, Serial Number 6 (Wilmington, NC: Broadfoot Publishing Company, 1996), p. 37.

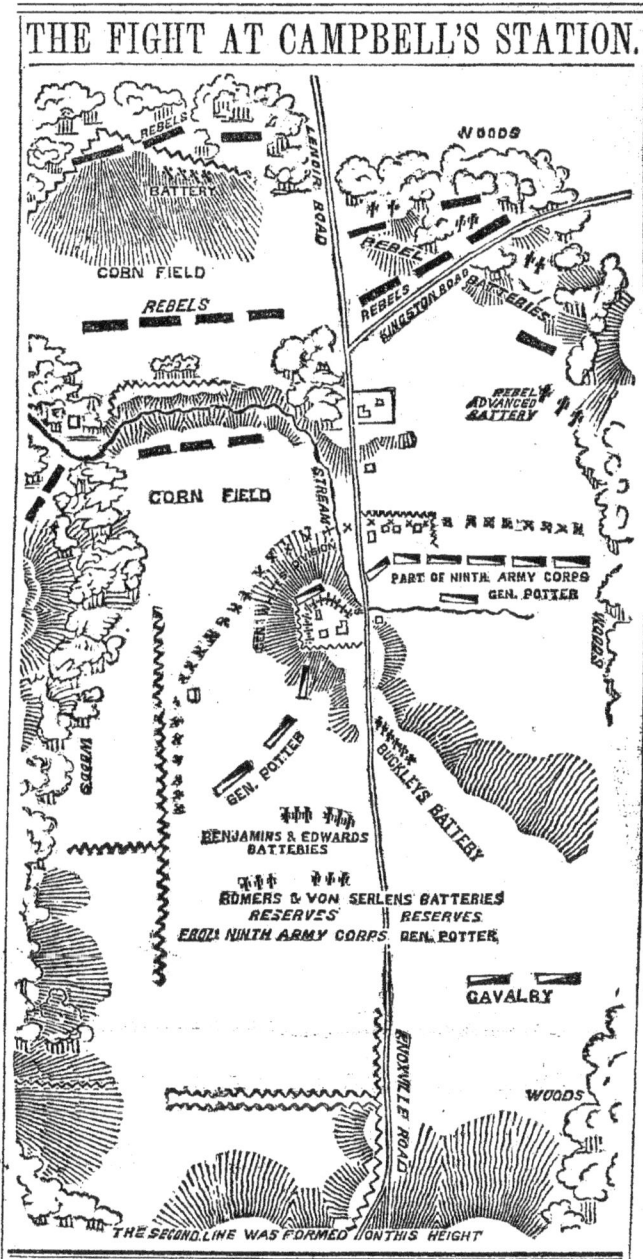

Figure 16
*Battle of Campbell's Station.* New York Tribune, December 7, 1863

The first Union line of battle, which formed in the middle of the valley, and the final stand, which formed behind the Concord Road, appear in this map to have occurred at the same time. The statement at the bottom of the map, 'The second line was formed on this height', gives the impression that Burnside's troops all retreated to his position before dark. Chapin's Brigade is referred to as 'Gen. White's Division', and the writing is concealed in the lines representing the sides of the plateau at the intersection of the Concord and Kingston Roads.

The 'L' shaped house to the left of the caption 'Rebel Advanced Battery' is the Campbell's Station Inn, which is now at the corner of Kingston Pike and Campbell's Station Road North. The buildings on the right side of the road just above the caption 'Part of Ninth Army Corps' are the William W. Nelson House and outbuildings. The buildings on the left of the road just below the above are the James Swan home and outbuildings. There are some other presumed buildings on the map to which no reference was made by soldiers, and the identification is now unknown.[16]

---

[16] Special Correspondent, 'The Fight at Campbell's Station', *New York Tribune*, 7 December 1863, from a copy in the author's collection.

# 9

## EPILOGUE

General Ambrose Burnside's forces successfully retreated into the defensive positions at Knoxville on 17 November 1863, the day after the Battle of Campbell's Station. With General Lafayette McLaws in the lead, the Southerners followed Burnside to Knoxville. Confederate General James Longstreet attacked and laid siege to Knoxville, culminating in the disastrous attack on Fort Sanders on November 29th. When word reached Longstreet that Confederates were defeated at Missionary Ridge in Chattanooga and Union General William T. Sherman was moving toward Knoxville with a large force, he retreated from Knoxville. The Confederates stayed and fought in upper east Tennessee during the winter of 1863-1864. In the spring of 1864 after a very hard winter in East Tennessee, Longstreet moved back to Virginia and rejoined General Robert E. Lee's Army of Northern Virginia.

General Ambrose Burnside, who had been ill with an intestinal problem for sometime, had requested to be relieved of command before Longstreet's advance. Ironically, the order for his replacement was issued on 16 November 1863 the day of the Battle of Campbell's Station. General John G. Foster, who was named to be Burnside's successor, arrived in Knoxville on 11 December 1863, and Burnside left the next day. On his way to Rhode Island, Burnside stopped in Cincinnati, Ohio, where he was called on to make a speech. 'General Burnside said that the honors his countrymen were bestowing upon him because of his East Tennessee Campaign belonged rather to his officers and men.' This statement was not just modesty, it was the truth. Without the almost superhuman efforts of the men in his command on the retreat, all could have been lost.[1]

From May through July 1865, two of the participants in the Battle of Campbell's Station played important roles in the trial and execution of the President Abraham Lincoln assassination conspirators. Major General John Hartranft, who had been a division commander in the battle, was appointed as the warden of the prison where the conspirators were held and tried. Seven men and one woman were on trial for the assassination of Lincoln, the attempted assassination of Secretary of State William Seward, and a plot to kill Vice President Andrew Johnson. Of the eight, George A. Atzerodt, Lewis Powell, David E. Herold, and Mary E. Surratt were sentenced to death by hanging. The other four were sentenced to prison terms.

In 1865 Captain Christian Rath formerly of Company G, 17th Michigan Infantry had been appointed to Hartranft's staff. In that capacity he had been designated to design and oversee the erection of the scaffold on which the convicted conspirators were hanged. Rath personally tied the nooses in the ropes for the hanging and placed the ropes around the necks of the condemned. He also gave the signal to perform the hanging of all four convicted conspirators at one time.[2]

Although the Confederates held the field after the Battle of Campbell's Station was over, which some might consider a victory, this was a very important victory for General Burnside and the Union cause. Burnside's objectives had been to move his troops to the relative safety of Knoxville's defenses, give the garrison in Knoxville time to prepare for a siege, draw Longstreet's men further away from Chattanooga, and keep Longstreet occupied while General Grant defeated the Confederates in Chattanooga. For the second time in two days, Burnside had successfully accomplished all of his objectives. The winner at the Battle of Campbell's Station had been the Army of the Ohio. Even Burnside's adversary Confederate General James Longstreet in his memoirs wrote that Burnside's 're-

---

[1] William Marvel, *Burnside* (Chapel Hill, NC: The University of North Carolina Press, 1991), p. 334; *The War of Rebellion*, Series 1, Volume 31, Part 3, p. 166; Henry S. Burrage, Henry S. 'Burnside's East Tennessee Campaign', *Papers of the Military Historical Society of Massachusetts* Volume VIII, (Boston, MA: The Military Historical Society of Massachusetts, 1910), p. 603.

[2] Gambone, *Major-General John Frederick Hartranft*, pp. 181-92.

treat was very cleverly conducted'.[3] No higher compliment could be made.

What if the Confederates had gotten to the junction first? Then the Federal forces may have been destroyed as a fighting unit, or if able to fight their way out of the trap, they would have been very much weakened. Thus, the Confederates may have captured Knoxville. Longstreet would not have had time to return to Chattanooga and help in the fight for that city. In early December just as he really did, Federal General William T. Sherman would have come up the valley to recapture Knoxville, and there would have been another siege of Knoxville with the Confederates on the inside this time. Confederates did not fair well when besieged. Several cases in point are: Fort Donelson, Tennessee, where the Confederates surrendered in February 1862; Arkansas Post, Arkansas, when the Confederates surrendered in January 1863; Vicksburg, Mississippi, which surrendered in July 1863; and Petersburg, Virginia, which was abandoned in April 1865 after months of siege.

---

[3] Longstreet, *From Manassas to Appomattox*, p. 492.

Figure 17
*Modern Day View of Burnside's Last Stand Area*
This photograph was taken from the approximate location as depicted in the Paul Long painting of the battle. The Nelson house is barely visible to the right of the McDonalds sign and above the white sign. The Campbell Station Inn is located in the clump of trees on the horizon, just to the right of the nearest utility pole.
From the Farragut Folklife Museum Collections.

**10**

## THE DEBRIS OF WAR:
## WHAT THE SOLDIERS LEFT BEHIND

After the soldiers left the Campbell's Station Battlefield, the debris they had produced remained. For decades the bullets, shells, buttons, and other military hardware that had been dropped or fired were left. Some were evidently plowed up and carried away, but most remained. Just prior to the rapid development of the battlefield area, men with the new technology of metal detectors saved many of these historical objects. One of the most dedicated researchers and probably the largest retriever of the relics was Jerry Keyes.

Before the Taco Bell, Krogers, housing developments, and scores of other businesses, Jerry Keyes was in the field recovering the buried artifacts. As a historian, researcher, and preservationist, Mr. Keyes has loaned part of his wonderful collection to the Farragut Folklife Museum. He is always forthcoming in sharing his knowledge of the battlefield and has been a wonderful resource to the author of this book.

What follows is a small part of the artifacts retrieved by Mr. Keyes using a metal detector beginning in the 1970's.

Figure 18
*3.67 Inch Schenkl Shell*

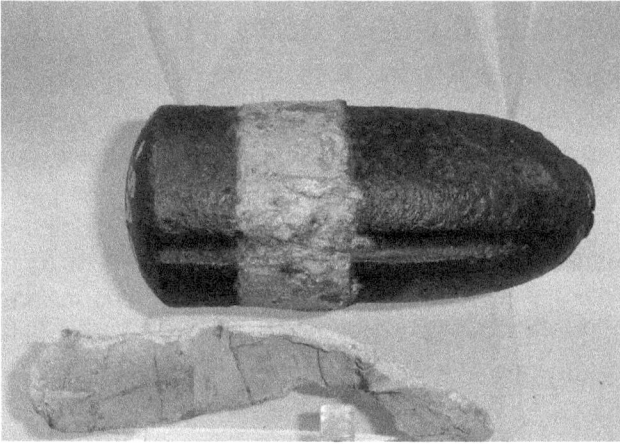

Figure 19
*3.8 Inch Hotckiss Shell with Sabot*

Figure 20
*3.8 Inch Hotckiss Shell with Writing*

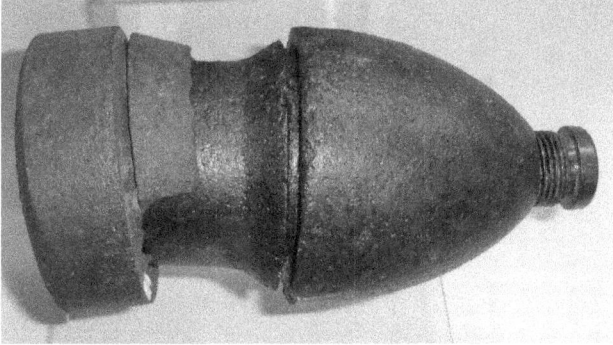

Figure 21
*3.8 Inch Hotckiss Shell*

Figure 22
*3.8 James Shell*

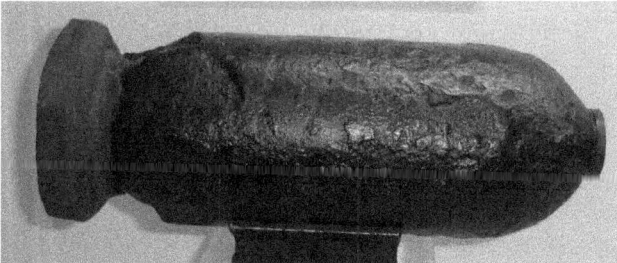

Figure 23
*20 Pounder Confederate Shell*

Figure 24
*Confederate 3 Inch Reed Shell*

Figure 25
*3 Inch Parrot Shell*

Figure 26
*This section of an oak tree originally stood in the front yard of the Dr. William Nelson home (the brick house behind the Taco Bell Restaurant) on 16 November 1863. In contains a Minie ball fired the day of the battle. The right hand arrow points to the location of the Minie ball, the middle arrow points to the place where the bullet struck the tree, and the horizontal arrow represents the tree's growth from 1863 until it was cut down.*

# Glossary of Mid-Nineteenth Century Military Words and Terms[1]

Words and terms printed in **Bold Face** within the definitions in this Glossary will have separate entries.

**Adjutant:** The Adjutant is a **Lieutenant** in the **Regiment** who is assigned by the colonel to assist him in issuing orders and other paper work.

**Ammunition:** Ammunition is the term referring to the powder, container, and projectile fired in a weapon. Almost all the ammunition used in the War was made in factories far behind the lines of the respective armies, and some of it was imported from overseas by both sides.

Ammunition for muzzle loading muskets, rifles, pistols, and rifle muskets was usually made with a paper cylinder or other combustible material containing the powder and the lead bullet either inside or partly exposed with the paper rapped around its base. In some types of ammunition, the paper was completely thrown away while loading, and in others it was kept around the bullet part only. In the case of pistols and breech loading carbines, the whole cartridge was placed in the cylinder and was consumed when the gun was fired.

---

[1] Information for this Glossary came primarily from the following sources: H.L. Scott, *Military Dictionary: Comprising Technical Definitions; On Raising and Keeping Troops; Actual Service, Including Makeshifts and Improved Materiel; and Law, Government, Regulation, and Administration Relating to Land Forces* (Yuma, Arizona: Fort Yuma Press, 1984 reprint of the 1864 edition); William Gilham, *Manual of Instruction for the Volunteers and Militia of the Confederate States* (Richmond, Virginia: West & Johnston, 1861); Frederick P. Todd, *American Military Equipage 1851-1872*, Volume I (Providence, Rhode Island: The Company of Military Historians, 1974); and Francis A. Lord, *Civil War Collector's Encyclopedia* (New York: Castle Books, 1965); Stanley S. Phillips, *Civil War Corps Badges and Other Related Awards, Badges, Medals of the Period* (published by the author, Lanham, Maryland, 1982); Warren Ripley, *Artillery and Ammunition of the Civil War* (New York, New York: Promontory Press, 1970).

Ammunition for breech loading weapons took several forms. Cartridges for such **Rifles** and **Carbines** as made by Sharps and others were self consuming when lighted by the percussion cap. Others had a metal case such as the Burnside and Maynard products containing the powder and had a small hole in the end opposite the bullet where the flame from the percussion cap ignited it. Still others, such as the Henry and Spencer carbines, used a rim fired cartridge that resembled a modern .22 caliber cartridge, only they were .44 and .52 caliber. Rim fired meant that there was a small amount of solid explosive (fulminate of mercury) around the rim of the bottom of the brass case that exploded and ignited the powder when it was struck by the firing pin.

A percussion cap was made of brass and looked like a hat with a brim and was coated with fulminate of mercury on the inside top of the hat. The percussion cap was placed on the cone of the weapon, and when struck by the hammer, the fulminate of mercury exploded and sent the flame down a tube to the powder charge thus firing the weapon. Usually twelve caps were issued with every ten cartridges.

All ammunition for **Artillery** weapons had the powder contained in a wool bag most often attached to the rear of the cannon projectile. There were many types of projectiles for cannons. Smooth bore cannon fired round balls and canister. The round balls could be solid iron, have a cavity inside which contained powder called a shot or a shell, or filled with powder and metal balls called a case or spherical shot. A canister was a thin metal can filled with small projectiles and no powder. When the canister was fired, the can blew apart creating a huge shotgun effect. Rifled cannon fired bullet-shaped projectiles were of the same makeup as the round balls and canister. The hollow projectiles were affixed with fuses that were lighted by the explosion of the powder as the projectile left the barrel. Only rifled cannon had a percussion fuse that would explode the shell when it hit a solid object.

**Armies:** Armies were usually made up of two or more **Corps** and were commanded by a General. The United States had at least 16 different armies, and the Confederacy had at least 23 armies at different times during the War. The U.S. Armies tended to be named for the river near where they were organized, such as the Army of the Tennessee or the Army of the Ohio. The C.S. armies tended to be named for the state or area in which they were first organized, such as the Army of Tennessee or the Army of Northern Virginia.

**Artillery:** Every type of large caliber cannons, guns, mortars, how-itzers, etc. are called artillery. Cannons are referred to by the weight of the solid shot fired, such as a 12 pounder or 24 pounder, and by the size of the gun's bore, such as a 3 inch rifle.

Heavy Artillery units worked the large caliber cannons that were used in forts or in attacking forts. Light, Field, or Horse Artillery units usually had the smaller caliber cannons pulled by horses or mules that could be moved with an army.

Cannons were made of iron and bronze and could be either smooth bore or rifled. While most of the cannons were muzzle loaders, there were a few breech loaders in use during the War. No breech loaded cannon were used in the Battle of Campbell's station. The uniforms of artillerymen were supposed to be trimmed in red cloth, and they were armed with swords, pistols, and various types of shoulder weapons.

James Rifle: This type of cannon was made of bonze 3.8 inch caliber cannon that usually had ten lands and grooves of rifling and fired a solid shot that weighted fourteen pounds. It was named for the inventor, Charles T. James, who was accidentally killed while experimenting with cannon projectiles in 1862.

Napoleon Cannon: This cannon was also known as a 12 Pound-er. It was a bronze 4.62 caliber smooth bore cannon that fired round projectiles and canister. The Napoleon was very popular with both the Union and Confederate armies. It was named for the French Emperor, Napoleon III, who was credited with having the cannon developed.

Parrott Rifles: The Parrott Rifles are very distinctive with a large iron reinforcing band at the breech. Two types of Parrott Rifles were used at Campbell's Station. The 10 Pounder size had either a 2.9 inch or 3 inch rifled bore. The 20 Pounder size had a 3.67 inch rifled bore. Both sizes fired long, bullet shaped projectiles. These cannons were invented, manufactured, and named for the inventor Robert P. Parrott.

6 Pounder Cannon: This was an iron or usually a bronze 3.67 caliber smooth bore cannon which fired round projectiles and can-ister.

12 Pounder Cannon: See Napoleon Cannon.

24 Pounder Cannon: This large field piece was a 5.82 caliber smooth bore cannon that fired round projectiles and canister. Usually, they were made of bronze, but some were made of iron.

3 Inch Rifle: This cannon was also known as 3 inch Ordnance Rifle. It is an iron, three inch rifled cannon that fired long bullet shaped projectiles.

**Battalion:** This was an organization of two through nine **Companies** serving under the same commander, usually a **Major** or **Lieutenant-Colonel**.

**Batteries:** Batteries were two or more, but usually four or six, cannons under the same commander. Although both sides had some regiments of **Artillery** with batteries with letter designations, both sides usually organized batteries as independent organizations. Confederate batteries were usually known by their commander's name, such as Parker's Virginia Battery. The northern counterparts usually had state designations, such as 2nd Rhode Island Battery. The battery was subdivided into sections usually consisting of two cannon to a section. Batteries often divided into sections with sections placed in different parts of the battlefield.

**Brigade:** A brigade was made up of two or more **Regiments** and usually was commanded by a **Brigadier General** or **Colonel**. Each side tended to average about four or five regiments to a brigade. As the War continued, they tended to contain more and more regiments as the regiments got smaller. In the Confederate Army, brigades were usually known by the commander's name. In the United States Army, brigades were usually referred to by the commander's name, and also numbers were used.

**Caisson:** A caisson was a two wheeled, wooden carriage that carried two cannon ammunition chests and had a spare wheel on the back. In order to move, it needed to be hooked to the rear of the two wheeled **Limber**.

**Caliber:** The diameter of the bore of small arms, such as pistols, rifles, muskets, and rifle muskets is referred to as its' caliber. A caliber is 1/100 of an inch; thus, a .50 caliber weapon fires a projectile that is ½ inch in diameter.

**Cannons:** See Artillery.

**Captain:** The captain was a commissioned officer in rank below a **Major** and above a **1ST Lieutenant.** In the **Artillery, Cavalry,** and **Infantry** he was in command of a **Company.** In the United States Army his rank was indicated by two silver bars on straps located on each shoulder of his coat. In the Confederate Army his rank was indicated by three horizontal gold stripes on each side of the collar of his coat.

**Carbine:** A carbine was a short, shoulder firearm, primarily used by the **Cavalry.** United States carbines were usually breechloaders. Confederates used captured carbines and sawed off muzzle loading shotguns, and they imported and manufactured some breech and muzzle loading carbines.

**Cavalry:** Cavalry were soldiers who were mounted on horses and trained to fight on horseback or on foot. The cavalrymen were armed with pistols, swords, and **Carbines.** Uniforms of cavalrymen were supposed to be trimmed in yellow cloth.

**Colonel:** A colonel was a commissioned officer in rank below a brigadier **General** and above a **Lieutenant Colonel.** In the **Artillery, Cavalry,** and **Infantry,** he was in command of a **Regiment.** Particularly in the Union army, a colonel could be in command of a **Brigade.** In the United States Army colonels were distinguished by stylized eagle designs on straps on each shoulder and by the button arrangement on their coats. Colonels in the Confederacy wore three gold stars on each side of the collar.

**Commissioned Officers:** These are the officers who had been officially appointed by the President. They included various grades of **General, Colonel, Lieutenant Colonel, Major, Captain,** and the different grades of **Lieutenant.** In **Regiments** raised by the states, the men usually elected their **Company** officers, and the **Company** officers then elected the **Field Officers** who were in turn confirmed by the President. Commissioned Officers could resign and leave the armed forces if they so desired. **Noncommissioned Officers** and **Privates** were discharged when the armed forces finished with them or their time of enlistment had ended.

**Company:** This was the basic unit of the army. It was supposed to have between 80 to 120 men. As the War progressed, these companies tended to get smaller and smaller in number. A company was supposed to be commanded by a **Captain** and supposed to have one **First Lieutenant**, one **Second Lieutenant**, one **First Sergeant**, four **Sergeants**, eight **Corporals**, two **Musicians**, one wagon driver, and about 65 to 105 **Privates.**

Each company was designated by a letter beginning with A going through the alphabet, except that there was usually never a Company J. The reason was that the letters I and J were too easily confused.

**Corporal:** This was the lowest rank of noncommissioned officers which was below the rank of **Sergeant** and above the rank of **Private.** In both armies Corporals were designated by two V shaped pieces of cloth on each shoulder in the color of their branch of service.

**Corps:** This was an army organization made up of at least two but usually three or more **Divisions**. Various grades of **Generals** commanded a Corps. A Corps would contain units of **Artillery, Cavalry**, and **Infantry**. United States Corps were numbered and usually were referred to by number, such as the 9^TH Corps and 23^rd Corps. The Confederate Corps were numbered but were usually known by their commander's name, such as Longstreet's 1^st Corps.

Cloth Corps Badges were developed in the United States Army during the War to help identify soldiers and to build morale. Later on, these Corps badges were made of all kinds of metal as well as cloth. The **Divisions** within a Corps had their badges in different colors. The 1^st Division was red, the 2^nd white, the 3^rd blue, 4^th green, and the 5^th orange.

The 9^th Corps badge was shield shaped with a cannon barrel and an anchor with rope. The anchor symbolized the landing on the coast of North Carolina. The badge for the 9^th Corps was not adopted until 10 April 1864, months after the Battle of Campbell's Station. The 23rd Corps' badge was not adopted until 25 September 1864, and the badge was a plain, a more rounded shield than the 9th Corps Badge.

Figure 27
*9th Corps Badge*

Figure 28
*23rd Corps Badge*

**Dismounted Cavalry: Cavalry** which for any number of reasons had no horses and fought on foot still retaining their cavalry weapons was called dismounted cavalry.

**Field Officers:** The regimental **Colonel, Lieutenant-Colonel,** and **Major** were field officers and were mounted, even in the **Infantry**.

**Flank:** This was a military unit's end of the line. The right and left flanks of the unit were based on the direction that the unit faced.

**Flanking:** This term was used to describe the enemy's attempt to attack the unit's Flank rear.

**Foot Officers:** The foot officers were the **Captains** and **Lieutenants** of **Infantry Regiments**.

**Generals:** They were the highest ranking **Commissioned Officers** and were above **Colonels**. During the War, there were four grades of generals in the Confederate Army and three in the United States Army. Beginning with the lowest to the highest, there were four types of generals: Brigadier General, Major General, Lieutenant General, General. In the United States Army they were identified by the number of gold stars on their shoulder straps: one star for Brigadier, two for a Major, three for a Lieutenant General. (Grant was the only Lieutenant General.) In the Confederate Army all generals, regardless of grade, were identified only by three gold stars surrounded by a gold wreath on each side of the collar.

**Infantry:** The infantry were soldiers who fought and marched on foot. If the soldiers' uniform was trimmed, the trim was blue, light blue in the United States uniforms and all shades of blue in the Confederate army.

**Legion:** During the War, this usually referred to a unit made up of **Infantry, Cavalry, and Artillery** or some combination of the three. By late 1863 most of the legions were only infantry. Confederate Hampton's Legion was one of the most famous during the War. Thomas' Confederate Legion fought and recruited men in this area. Phillips' Georgia Legion fought at Campbell's Station.

**Lieutenant:** There were 1$^{st}$ and 2$^{nd}$ Lieutenants. The 1$^{st}$ Lieutenant was the higher rank. Lieutenants were in rank below the rank of

**Captain** and were the lowest grade of the **Commissioned Offic-ers.** In the United States Army, 1st Lieutenants were identified by a gold bar on each end of his shoulder straps, and a 2nd Lieutenant had no insignia on his shoulder strap. In the Confederate army the 1st Lieutenant had two gold bars on each collar, and a 2nd Lieutenant had one gold bar on each side of the collar.

**Limber:** This was a two wheeled cart that held a single ammunition chest for a cannon. It had a hook at the rear to which a cannon, **Caisson**, or portable forge could be attached for movement.

**Line of Battle:** The Line of Battle was the usual method of fighting and consisted of the soldiers in two lines facing in the same direc-tion. In the infantry there was supposed to be only sixteen inches between the lines with their elbows touching the elbows of the men on either side of them. The first line was the front rank, and the line behind them was the rear rank. The men in the rear rank aimed and fired their weapons to the right of the man in the front rank.

**Major:** A Major was a **Commissioned Officer** between the rank of **Lieutenant-Colonel** and **Captain**. In the United States Army a major wore gold leaves on each end of his shoulder strap. In the Confederate Army his insignia was one gold star on each side of the collar.

**Mounted Infantry:** These were **Infantry** soldiers who retained their infantry weapons but moved from one location to another riding horses or mules. On arriving at a battle, they dismounted and fought on foot.

**Musket:** This was a military shoulder arm that had no rifling in the barrel. It is called a smoothbore. Most muskets used in the War were .69 caliber and could be as large as .75 caliber in some foreign-made imported models. Many old flintlock muskets were used in the first part of the War. Flintlocks converted to percussion and percussion muskets continued to be used the entire War, especially in the Confederate Army.

**Non-Commissioned Officers:** They were ranked between the **Commissioned Officers** and **Privates.** There were two grades of non-commissioned officers: **Sergeants**, being higher, and **Corporals**. Sergeants could wear three v-shaped (points down) chevrons in branch of service color on each sleeve. Corporals wore two chevrons.

**Privates:** This was the lowest rank in the military and made up the bulk of the army. Unlike today, the Private wore no insignia of rank.

**Regiments:** Infantry regiments were composed of ten **Companies** and **Cavalry** and **Heavy Artillery** of twelve companies. Most regiments on both sides were designated by state names, such as the 2$^{nd}$ Tennessee Infantry Regiment. There were troops raised by both the Confederate and United States governments that went by such names as the 4$^{th}$ Confederate Infantry or 15$^{th}$ United States Infantry. Some states, such as Tennessee, who raised troops for both sides, often are designated by (US) or (CS) after the name of the regiment by modern writers, but was not used during the War.

The word 'Volunteers' is often used in regimental names and has several meanings. Some units used the term to designate that they were volunteers rather than drafted men. In the Union Army they were officially designated as Volunteers if they reenlisted as a regiment after their first enlistment had expired.

Regiments were usually led by **Field Officers**, but as can be seen in the Order of Battle, some were lead by Captains.

**Rifle:** These shoulder arms were usually made in the same calibers as the **Rifle Muskets**. Rifles had shorter, thicker barrels and deeper rifling than the rifle musket. Some early rifles were made in .54 caliber. In theory, the rifle could fire a larger amount of powder, but in practice, they used the same ammunition as the Rifle Musket. Also included in this category were a number of breech loading arms that were fired by percussion caps and a few that used a rim fired cartridge.

**Rifle Musket:** Rifle musket was the official name given to the shoulder weapon most commonly used in the War. The most common calibers of Rifle Muskets were .577 (British made 'Enfields'), .58 caliber for the various models of the standard United States arms, and .54 caliber in the imported Austrian Lorenz.

**Skirmish Line:** The skirmish line was a single line of soldiers with several feet distance between the men. One **Company** of a **Regiment** usually served as the skirmish line for the regiment. The skirmish line was usually deployed a hundred to several hundred yards in advance of the **Line of Battle** whether advancing, retreating, or stationary. The skirmish line served as an early warning system for the **Line of Battle**. If the enemy was in a large force, the skirmishers were to fire and retreat back to their larger forces. In the Battle of Campbell's Station, the 45th Pennsylvania Infantry was used as skirmishers for the rest of the brigade, and Chapin's Brigade acted as skirmishers for the rest of the Army of the Ohio.

# Appendix A

## Order of Battle[1]
## Campbell's Station, Tennessee
## 16 November 1863

### Union Forces

### Army of the Ohio
Major General Ambrose E. Burnside, Commanding

### 9th Army Corps
Brigadier General Robert B. Potter, Commanding

First Division
Brigadier General Edward Ferrero, Commanding

First Brigade
Colonel David Morrison, Commanding

36th Massachusetts, Major William E. Draper
8th Michigan, Lt. Colonel Ralph Ely
79th New York, Captain William S. Montgomery
45th Pennsylvania, Lt. Colonel Francis M. Hills

---

[1] The primary information of the Union and Confederate Troops at the Battle of Campbell's Station was obtained from the following sources:
Orlando Poe, 'The Defense of Knoxville', in Robert U. Johnson and Clarence C. Buel, *Battles and Leaders of the Civil War*, Volume III (New York: The Century Company, 1888), pp. 751-52; Stewart Sifakis, *Compendium of the Confederate States, Alabama* (1992), *Louisiana* (1995), *South Carolina and Georgia* (1995), *Virginia* (1992), (New York, NY: Facts On File); *The War of Rebellion*, Series I, Volume 31, Part 1, pp. 288-90, 451-54; *The War of Rebellion*, Series I, Volume 31, Part 2, pp. 657-58.

Second Brigade
Colonel Benjamin C. Christ, Commanding

29th Massachusetts, Colonel Ebenezer W. Peirce
27th Michigan, Major William B. Wright
46th New York, Captain Alphons Serieri
50th Pennsylvania, Major Edward Overton, Jr.

Third Brigade
Colonel William Humphrey, Commanding

2nd Michigan, Major Corenlius Byington
17th Michigan, Lt. Colonel Lorin L. Comstock
20th Michigan, Colonel William Huntington Smith, Killed in Action
Major Byron M. Cutcheon took command at Smith's death
Companies A, B and F 100th Pennsylvania, Captain Thomas J.
Hamilton

34th New York Artillery, Captain Jacob Roemer
Company D, 1st Rhode Island Artillery, Captain William W. Buckley

Second Division
Colonel John F. Hartranft, Commanding

First Brigade,
Colonel Joshua K. Siegfried, Commanding

2nd Maryland, Colonel Thomas B. Allard
21st Massachusetts, Lt. Colonel George P. Hawkes
48th Pennsylvania, Major Joseph A. Gilmour

Second Brigade[2]
Lt. Colonel Edwin Schall, Commanding

---

[2] The 11th New Hampshire Infantry which was usually in the Schall's Second Brigade, Second Division, 9th Corps was stationed in Knoxville on 16 November 1863. Leander W. Cogswell, *A History of the Eleventh New Hampshire Regiment Volunteer Infantry in the Rebellion War, 1861-1865* (Memphis, TN: General Books, 2010), pp. 74-75; Janet B. Hewett (ed.), *Supplement to the Official Records of the Union and Confederate Armies* (Serial Number 51; Wilmington, NC: Broadfoot Publishing Company, 1996), pp. 434-57.

35<sup>th</sup> Massachusetts, Major Nathaniel Wales
51<sup>st</sup> Pennsylvania, Major William J. Bolton

Battery E, 2<sup>nd</sup> U. S. Artillery, 1<sup>st</sup> Lieutenant Samuel N. Benjamin
Batteries L and M consolidated, 3<sup>rd</sup> U. S. Artillery, 1<sup>st</sup> Lieutenant
Erskine Gittings

## 23<sup>rd</sup> Army Corps

Second Division
Brigadier General Julius White, Commanding

Second Brigade
Colonel Marshall W. Chapin, Commanding

107<sup>th</sup> Illinois, Colonel Joseph J. Kelly[3]
13<sup>th</sup> Kentucky, Colonel William E. Hobson
23<sup>rd</sup> Michigan, Major William Wheeler
111<sup>th</sup> Ohio, Major Isaac C. Sherwood

Henshaw's Independent Illinois Light Artillery, Captain Edward C.
Henshaw

Cavalry and Mounted Infantry
Colonel James Biddle, Commanding

112<sup>th</sup> Illinois Mounted Infantry, Major Tristram T. Dow
Companies A, B, G, and K, 6<sup>th</sup> Indiana Cavalry, Colonel James Biddle[4]
8<sup>th</sup> Michigan Cavalry, Major Henry C. Edgerly

---

[3] Colonel Kelly was scheduled to take a leave of absence on 14 November 1863, but with Confederates arriving choose to stay with his regiment. Moore, *The Rebellion Record*, p. 273.

[4] Hewett, *Supplement to the Official Records of the Union and Confederate Armies*, Serial 27, p. 359.

Reserve Artillery

15th Indiana Artillery, Captain John C. H. Von Sehlen
24th Indiana Light Artillery, Captain Joseph A. Sims

The primary information of the Union Troops at the Battle of Campbell's Station was obtained from the following sources:
Orlando Poe, 'The Defense of Knoxville', Robert U. Johnson and Clarence C. Buel, *Battles and Leaders of the Civil War*, Volume III (New York: The Century Company, 1888), pp. 751-52; United States War Department: *The War of the Rebellion: A Compilation of the Official Records of the Union and Confederate Armies* (Harrisburg, PA: The National Historical Society, 1971), Volume 31, Part 1, pp. 267, 811-816.

## CONFEDERATE FORCES

### First Corps, Army of Northern Virginia
Lt. General James Longstreet, Commanding

McLaws' Division
Major General Lafayette McLaws, Commanding

Kershaw' Brigade
Brigadier General Joseph B. Kershaw, Commanding

2nd South Carolina, Colonel John D. Kennedy
3rd South Carolina, Colonel James D. Nance
7th South Carolina, Captain Elijah J. Goggans[5]
8th South Carolina, Colonel John W. Henagan
15th South Carolina, Major William M. Gist
3rd South Carolina Battalion Sharpshooters, Lt. Colonel William G.

---

[5] The 7th South Carolina was led by only a Captain due to the death or resignation of all the field officers. Roger Seiger, *South Carolina's Military Organizations During the War Between the States* (Charleston, SC: The History Press, 2008), Volume II, page 170-71.

Rice

Wofford's Brigade
Colonel Solon Z. Ruff, Commanding[6]

16th Georgia, Lt. Colonel Henry P. Thomas
18th Georgia, Captain John A. Crawford
24th Georgia, Captain N. J. Dorth
Cobb's Georgia Legion, Major William D. Conyers
Phillips' Georgia Legion, Major Joseph Hamilton
3rd Georgia Battalion Sharpshooters, Lt. Colonel Nathan L. Hutchins

Humphrey's Brigade
Brigadier General Benjamin G. Humphrey, Commanding

13th Mississippi, Colonel Kennon McElroy
17th Mississippi, Lt. Colonel John C. Fiser
18th Mississippi, Colonel Thomas M. Griffen
21st Mississippi, Colonel William L. Brandon

Bryan's Brigade
Brigadier General Goode Bryan, Commanding

10th Georgia, Lt. Colonel Willis C. Holt
50th Georgia, Lt. Colonel Peter A. S. McGlashan
51st Georgia, Colonel Edward Ball
53rd Georgia, Colonel James P. Simms

---

[6] Brigadier General William T. Wofford was on leave due to illness and absent from his brigade during November and December 1863. Colonel Solon Z. Ruff was killed at Fort Sanders on 29 November 1863. Due to the temporary absence of General Wofford the brigade will be referred to as Wofford's in this book. Davis, *The Confederate General*, Volume 6, p. 157; Welsh, *Medical Histories of Confederate Generals*, p. 239; Bruce S. Allardice, *Confederate Colonels: A Biographical Register* (Columbia, MO: University of Missouri Press, 2008), p. 329.

Jenkins' Division[7]
Brigadier General Micah Jenkins, Commanding[8]


Bratton's Brigade,[9]
Colonel John Bratton, Commanding


1st South Carolina, Captain James R. Hagood[10]
2nd South Carolina Rifles, Colonel Thomas Thomson
5th South Carolina, Colonel Asbury Coward
6th South Carolina, Lt. Colonel John M. Steedman
Hampton's South Carolina Legion Battalion, Colonel Martin W.
Gary
South Carolina Palmetto Sharpshooters, Colonel Joseph Walker


Law's Brigade
Brigadier General Evander McIver Law, Commanding


4th Alabama, Colonel Pinkney D. Bowles

---

[7] Most sources list Brigadier General Jerome B. Robertson's Brigade as being at Campbell's Station, but they had been sent back to Loudon and Lenoir's Station to 'keep things in order there and take charge of the bridge'. Simpson, *Hood's Texas Brigade*, p. 351; John C. West, *A Texan in Search of a Fight, Being the Diary and Letters of a Private Soldier in Hood's Texas Brigade* (Baltimore, MD: Butternut and Blue, 1994), pp. 130-34.

[8] Jenkins' Division is often referred to as Hood's Division. General John Bell Hood had been the commander until his right leg had to be amputated because of a wound received in the Battle of Chickamauga, 20th September 1863. For clarity in this history, the unit will always be titled Jenkins' Division. Welsh, *Medical Histories of Confederate Generals*, p. 105.

[9] Bratton's Brigade is often referred to as Jenkin's Brigade in original sources. When Jenkins was promoted to division command, Bratton took command of Jenkin's old brigade. No one knew in the fall of 1863 that General Hood would not return to this division, thus the retention of the original names. For clarity in this history, the unit will always be titled Bratton's Brigade.

[10] The 1st South Carolina's Colonel Franklin W. Kilpatrick is often found as leading this regiment in many sources, but he had been killed on 28 October 1863 at the Battle of Wauhatchie. The Lt. Colonel and Major were both regarded as incompetent and may not have been with the regiment. Captain John R. Hagood was officially promoted from Captain to Colonel to date from 16 November 1863 the date of the Battle of Campbell's Station. The assumption has been made that in fact Hagood was leading the regiment in the battle. Robert S. Seige, *South Carolina's Military Organizations During the War Between the States*, 4 Volumes (Charleston, SC: The History Press, 2008), Volume II, p. 54.

15th Alabama, Major Alexander A. Lowther[11]
44th Alabama, Colonel William F. Perry
47th Alabama, Colonel Michael J. Bulger[12]
48th Alabama, Colonel James L. Sheffield

Anderson's Brigade
Brigadier General George T. Anderson, Commanding

7th Georgia, Colonel William P. White
8th Georgia, Colonel John R. Towers
9th Georgia, Colonel Benjamin Beck
11th Georgia, Colonel F. H. Little
59th Georgia, Lt. Colonel Bolivar H. Gee[13]

Benning's Brigade
Brigadier General Henry L. Benning

2nd Georgia, Colonel Edgar M. Butt
15th Georgia, Colonel Dudley M. Du Bose
17th Georgia, Colonel Wesley C. Hodges
20th Georgia, Colonel James D. Waddell

Artillery
Colonel E. Porter Alexander, Commanding

---

[11] The 15th Alabama's Colonel William C. Oates is usually listed as in command of his regiment in November 1863, but should be Major Alexander A. Lowther. Oates was severely wounded on 28 October 1863 at the Battle of Wauhatie, just south of Chattanooga. Oates did not return to his regiment until March 1864. Glenn W. LaFantasie, *Gettysburg Requiem: The Life and Lost Causes of Confederate William C. Oates* (New York, NY: Oxford University Press, 2006), pp. 150, 153.

[12] The 47th Alabama is usually listed as being commanded by Colonel Michael J. Bulger in the fall of 1863. Bulger had been captured in July 1863 and was not exchanged until March 1864. Bruce S. Allardice, *Confederate Colonels: A Biographical Register* (Columbia, MO: University of Missouri Press, 2008), p. 81.

[13] The 59th Georgia's commander is generally listed as Colonel William A.J. 'Jack' Brown. Brown was captured in July 1863 and was not exchanged until March 1864. Allardice, *Confederate Colonels*, p. 79.

9[14]<sup></sup>
9<sup>th</sup> Georgia (Leyden's) Battalion[14]
Major Austin Leyden, Commanding

Battery C, Captain Andrew M. Wolihin
Battery D, Captain Tyler M. Peeples

Alexander's Battalion
Major Frank Huger, Commanding

Louisiana Battery, Captain George V. Moody
South Carolina Battery, Captain W. W. Fickling
Bedford Virginia Battery, Captain Tyler C. Jordon
Richmond Virginia Battery, Captain William M. Parker
Bath Virginia Battery, Captain Osmond B. Taylor
Ashland Virginia Battery, Captain Pichegru Woolfolk, Jr.

Cavalry

Hart's Cavalry Brigade[15]
Colonel John R. Hart, Commanding

1<sup>st</sup> Georgia, Lt. Colonel Samuel W. Davitte
3<sup>rd</sup> Georgia, Lt. Colonel Robert Thompson
4<sup>th</sup> Georgia Colonel Isaac W. Avery
6<sup>th</sup> Georgia, Major Benjamin F. Brown
Captain Jannedine H. Wiggin's Arkansas Battery

---

[14] Battery E, Captain Billington W. York's Battery E had moved to Loudon with this battalion, but due to the lack of animals the guns and equipment had to be left at Loudon. This battery eventually was captured by Sherman's troops at Loudon in December 1863. *The War of Rebellion*, Series 1, Volume 31, Part 3, p. 707; Chickamauga National Military Park, Marker for York's Battery.

[15] John Poole, *Cracker Cavaliers: The 2nd Georgia Cavalry Under Wheeler and Forrest* (Macon, GA: Mercer University Press, 2000), pp. 101-102.

# Appendix B

## Casualties in the Union Army of the Ohio

### 9th Corps

| Burnside's Escort | Killed | Wounded | Missing | Totals |
|---|---|---|---|---|
| 6th Indiana Cavalry (4 companies) | 0 | 0 | 2 | 2 |
| Totals | 0 | 0 | 2 | 2 |
| | | | | |
| Ferrero's 1st Division | | | | |
| Morrison's 1st Brigade | | | | |
| 36th Massachusetts | 4 | 16 | 5 | 25 |
| 8th Michigan | 0 | 14 | 0 | 14 |
| 79th New York | 0 | 0 | 0 | 0 |
| 45th Pennsylvania | 0 | 8 | 10 | 18 |
| Totals | 4 | 38 | 15 | 57 |
| | | | | |
| Christ's 2nd Brigade | | | | |
| 29th Massachusetts | 0 | 0 | 1 | 1 |
| 27th Michigan | 2 | 5 | 10 | 17 |
| 46th New York | 0 | 0 | 3 | 3 |
| 50th Pennsylvania | 1 | 5 | 0 | 6 |
| Totals | 3 | 10 | 14 | 27 |
| | | | | |
| Humphrey's 3rd Brigade | | | | |
| 2nd Michigan | 3 | 27 | 2 | 32 |
| 17th Michigan | 7 | 51 | 15 | 73 |
| 20th Michigan | 3 | 30 | 4 | 37 |
| 100th Pennsylvania | 0 | 3 | 0 | 3 |
| Totals | 13 | 111 | 21 | 145 |
| | | | | |
| Hartrantf's 2nd Division | | | | |
| Sigfried's 1st Brigade | | | | |
| 2nd Maryland | 0 | 0 | 4 | 4 |
| 21st Massachusetts | 0 | 0 | 0 | 0 |
| 48th Pennsylvania | 1 | 1 | 2 | 4 |
| Totals | 1 | 1 | 6 | 8 |

| Artillery | Killed | Wounded | Missing | Totals |
|---|---|---|---|---|
| Battery L, 2nd New York | 0 | 2 | 0 | 2 |
| Battery D, 1st Rhode Island | 0 | 1 | 0 | 1 |
| Totals | 0 | 3 | 0 | 3 |

| Schall's 2nd Brigade | | | | |
|---|---|---|---|---|
| 35th Massachusetts | 0 | 3 | 1 | 4 |
| 51st Pennsylvania | 0 | 3 | 0 | 3 |
| Totals | 0 | 6 | 1 | 7 |

| Artillery | | | | |
|---|---|---|---|---|
| Battery E, 2nd United States | 0 | 0 | 0 | 0 |
| Totals for 9th Corps | 21 | 169 | 59 | 249 |

## 23rd Corps

| Chapin's 2nd Brigade | Killed | Wounded | Missing | Totals |
|---|---|---|---|---|
| 107th Illinois | 0 | 3 | 0 | 3 |
| 13th Kentucky | 0 | 9 | 5 | 14 |
| 23rd Michigan | 8 | 23 | 8 | 39 |
| 111th Ohio | 0 | 5 | 0 | 5 |
| Totals | 8 | 40 | 13 | 61 |

| Artillery | | | | |
|---|---|---|---|---|
| Henshaw's Illinois | 2 | 0 | 0 | 2 |
| 24th Indiana | 0 | 1 | 0 | 1 |
| Totals | 2 | 1 | 0 | 3 |

| 1st Calvary Division 2nd Brigade | | | | |
|---|---|---|---|---|
| 112th Illinois Mounted Infantry | 0 | 1 | 23 | 24* |
| 8th Michigan | 0 | 0 | 1 | 1 |
| Totals | 0 | 1 | 24 | 25 |
| Totals for 23rd Corps | 10 | 42 | 37 | 89* |

| Grand Totals for the Army of the Ohio | | | | |
|---|---|---|---|---|
| 9th Corps | 21 | 169 | 59 | 249 |
| 23rd Corps | 10 | 42 | 37 | 89* |
| Grand Total | 31 | 211 | 96 | 338 |

* For unknown reasons *The Official Records of the War of the Rebellion* did not count the twenty men captured under Sergeant Solomon Dixon of Company C, 112th Illinois Mounted Infantry, but have been placed in these totals.

The above information has been taken from: United States War Department: *The War of the Rebellion: A Compilation of the Official Records of the Union and Confederate Armies* (Harrisburg, PA: The National Historical Society, 1971, Volume 31, Part 1, pp. 288-90. With information on the losses of the 112th Illinois Mounted Infantry from: Bradford F. Thompson. *History of the 112th Regiment of Illinois Volunteer Infantry in the Great War of the Rebellion 1862-1865*, The Stark County News Office, Toulon, Illinois, 1885, pp. 457-59.

# Appendix C

## Casualties in Longstreet's 1st Corps
## Army of Northern Virginia

|  | Killed | Wounded | Total |
|---|---|---|---|
| Jenkin's Division |  |  |  |
| Anderson's Brigade | 3 | 34 | 34 |
| Bratton's Brigade | 18 | 106 | 124 |
| Law's Brigade | 1 | 12 | 13 |
| Totals for Division | 22 | 152 | 174 |

This was the only official number of casualties found in this study the Battle of Campbell's Station. No reports of casualties were found for McLaws' Infantry Division nor the cavalry or artillery.

United States War Department: *The War of the Rebellion: A Compilation of the Official Records of the Union and Confederate Armies,* The National Historical Society, Harrisburg, Pennsylvania, Volume 31, Part 1, 1971, p. 526.

# BIBLIOGRAPHY

Alexander, Edward Porter, *Fighting for the Confederacy: The Personal Recollections of General Edward Porter Alexander* (Chapel Hill, NC: The University of North Carolina Press, 1989).

Albert, Allen D. (ed.), *History of the Forty-Fifth Regiment Pennsylvania Veteran Volunteer Infantry 1861-1865* (Williamsport, PA: Grit Publishing Company, 1912).

Allardice, Bruce S., *Confederate Colonels: A Biographical Register* (Columbia, MO: University of Missouri Press, 2008).

Angel, Margaret, *Not So Long Ago in the Concord-Farragut Area*, (Nashville, TN: Williams Printing Company, 1986).

Arliskas, Thomas M., *Cadet Gray and Butternut Brown: Notes on Confederate Uniforms* (Gettysburg, PA: Thomas Publications, 2006).

Augustus, Gerald L., *The Loudon County Area of East Tennessee in the War 1861-1865* (Paducah, KY: Turner Publishing Company, 2000).

Baldwin, James J., *The Struck Eagle: A Biography of Brigadier General Micah Jenkins* (Shippensburg, PA: Burd Street Press, 1996).

Beyer, W.F. and O.F. Keydel, *Deeds of Valor: How American's Civil War Heroes Won the Congressional Medal of Honor* (New York, NY: Smithmark Publishers, 2000).

Blackburn, George M., (ed.), *The Diary of Captain Ralph Ely of the Eighth Michigan Infantry* (Mount Pleasant, MI: Central Michigan University Press, 1965).

Bolton, William J., Richard A. Sauers (ed.), *The Civil War Journal of Colonel William J. Bolton, 51ˢᵗ Pennsylvania, April 20, 1861 – August 2, 1865* (Conshohocken, PA: Combined Publishing, 2000).

Bosbyshell, Oliver C., *The 48ᵗʰ in the War: Being a Narrative of the Campaigns of the 48ᵗʰ Regiment, Infantry, Pennsylvania Veteran Volunteers during the War of the Rebellion* (Philadelphia, PA: Avil Print Company, 1895).

Brearley, William Henry, *Recollections of the East Tennessee Campaign* (Detroit, MI: Tribune Book and Job Office, 1871).

Burns, James, 'The Hiwassee East Tennessee and Georgia Railroad', *The Daily Post-Athenian, Sesqui-Centennial Edition*, (Athens, Tennessee: 10 June 1969).

Burrage, Henry S., *History of the Thirty-Sixth Regiment Massachusetts Volunteers, 1862-1865* Boston MA: Press of Rockwell and Churchill, 1884).

Burrage, Henry S., 'How I Recovered My Sword', in *Military Order of the Loyal Legion of the United States* (Wilmington, NC: Broadfoot Publishing Company, 1992).

Burrage, Henry S., 'Burnside's East Tennessee Campaign', *Papers of the Military Historical Society of Massachusetts*, Volume VIII (Boston, MA: The Military Historical Society of Massachusetts, 1910).

Bush, Arthur J and Margaret S., *Black Power to Black Gold: The life and Times of William E. Hobson* Bowling Green, KY: A.J. and M.S. Bush, 1990).

Carruth, Summer, *History of the Thirty-Fifth Regiment, Massachusetts, Volunteers* (Boston, MA: Mills, Knight & Co., Printers, 1884).

Childs, Charles L. and Mary Lyn, (eds), *Green Corn, Fresh Beef, and Sick Flour: The Civil War Diary of Corporal Elijah L. Halsted* (Independence, MO: Blue & Grey Book Shoppe, 1999).

Cogswell, Leander W., *A History of the Eleventh New Hampshire Regiment Volunteer Infantry in the Rebellion War, 1861-1865* (Memphis, TN: General Books, 2010).

Coker, James Lide, *History of Company G, Ninth S.C. Regiment, Infantry, S.C. Army and of Company E, Sixth S.C. Regiment, Infantry, S.C. Army* (Greenwood, SC: The Attic Press, Inc., 1979) reprint of the original.

Cutcheon, Byron, *The Story of the Twentieth Michigan Infantry, July 15th, 1862 to May 30th, 1865* (Lansing, MI: Robert Smith Printing Company, 1904).

Cutcheon, Byron M., 'Recollections of Burnside's East Tennessee Campaign of 1863', in *Military Order of the Loyal Legion of the United States*, Volume 43 (Wilmington, NC: Broadfoot Publishing Company, 1993).

Daiss, Timothy, *In the Saddle: Exploits of the 5th Georgia Cavalry* (Atglen, PA: Schiffer Publishing, 1999).

Davis, Burke, *The Civil War: Strange & Fascinating Facts* (New York, NY: Wings Books, 1982).

Davis, William C. (ed.), *The Confederate General*, 6 Volumes (Harrisbueg, PA: National Historical Society, 1991).

Dawson, Francis W., *Reminiscences of Confederate Service 1861-1865* (Baton Rouge, LA: Louisiana State University Press, 1980 reprint of the 1882 edition).

Derry, Joseph T. (ed.), *Confederate Military History Extended Edition, Volume VII, Georgia* (Wilmington, NC: Broadfoot Publishing Company, 1987).

Dickert, D. Augustus, *History of Kershaw's Brigade* (Wilmington, NC: Broadfoot Publishing Company, 1990 reprint of the 1899 edition).

Dolzall, Gary W., 'Muddy, Soggy Race to Campbell's Station', *America's Civil War Magazine*, July 2002.

Dyer, Frederick, *A Compendium of the War of the Rebellion* (Dayton, OH: The Press of Morningside Bookshop, 1978 reprint of the 1908 edition).

Evans, William M., 'The Artillery at Knoxville', *Confederate Veteran Magazine*, Volume XXXI, (Wilmington, NC: Broadfoot Publishing Company, 1988).

Fitzpatrick, James C., 'Dispatches', *The New York Herald*, December 6, 1863.

Fout, Fredrick W., *The Dark Days of the Civil War, 1861 to 1865* (Lexington, KY: Forgotten Books, 2012, a reprint of the original 1904 edition).

Fox, Wells B., *What I Remember of the Great Rebellion* (Lansing, MI: Darius D. Throrp, 1892).

Gambone, A.M., *Major-General John Frederick Hartranft: Citizen Soldier and Pennsylvania Statesman* (Baltimore, MD: Butternut and Blue, 1995).

Gavin, William Gilfillan, *Campaigning With the Roundheads: The History of the Hundredth Pennsylvania Veteran Volunteer Infantry Regiment in the American Civil War 1861-1865* (Dayton, OH: Morningside House, Inc., 1989).

Gavin, William G. (ed.), *Infantry Pettit: The Civil War Letters of Corporal Frederick Pettit* Shippenburg, PA: White Mane Publishing Company, 1990).

Genco, James G. (compiler), *Arming Michigan's Regiments 1862-1864* (J.G. Genco, 1982).

Gilham, William, *Manual of Instruction for the Volunteers and Militia of the Confederate States* (Richmond, VA: West & Johnston, 1861).

Goree, Thomas J., *Longstreet's Aide: The Civil War Letters of Major Thomas J. Goree* (Charlottesville, VA: University Press of Virginia, 1995).

Grose, W. Todd, *Mountain Rebels: East Tennessee Confederates and the Civil War, 1860-1870* (Knoxville, TN: The University of Tennessee Press, 1999).

Hallock, Judith Lee, *General James Longstreet in the West: A Monumental Failure* (Fort Worth, TX: Ryan Place Publishers, 1995).

Halstead, Elijah L., Charles L. and Mary L. Childs (eds.), *Green Corn, Fresh Beef and Sick Flour, The Civil War Diary of Corporal Elijah L. Halstead* (Independence, MO: Blue & Grey Book Shoppe, 1999).

Henderson, Lillian (compiler), *Roster of the Confederate Soldiers of Georgia 1861-1865*, 6 Volumes (Hapeville, GA: Longino & Porter, Inc., 1955-1964).

Hess, Earl J., *The Knoxville Campaign: Burnside and Longstreet in East Tennessee* (Knoxville, TN: The University of Tennessee Press, 2012).

Hewett, Janet B. (ed.), *Supplement to the Official Records of the Union and Confederate Armies*, 100 Volumes (Wilmington, NC: Broadfoot Publishing Company, 1994-2001).

Hitchcock, George A., Ronald Watson (ed.), *From Ashby to Andersonville: The Civil War Diary and Reminiscences of Private George A. Hitchcock, 21st Massachusetts Infantry* (Campbell, CA: Savas Publishing Company, 1997).

Klein, Maury, 'The Knoxville Campaign', *Civil War Times Illustrated* Vol. 10 (October 1971), pp. 4-11.

Krick, Robert E.L., *Staff Officers in Gray* (Chapel Hill, NC: The University of North Carolina, 2003).

Krick, Robert K., *Parker's Virginia Battery C.S.A.* (Berryville, VA: Virginia Book Company, 1975).

Krick, Robert K., *Lee's Colonels* (Dayton, OH: Morningside House, Inc., 1992).

LaFantasie, Glenn W., *Gettysburg Requiem: The Life and Lost Causes of Confederate William C. Oates* (New York, NY: Oxford University Press, 2006).

Laine, J. Gary and Morris M. Penny, *Law's Alabama Brigade in the War Between the Union and the Confederacy* (Shippensburg, PA: White Mane Publishing Co., 1996).

Lane, David, *A Soldier's Diary: The Story of a Volunteer, 1862-1865* Jackson, MI: David Lane, 1905).

Lewis, Richard, *Camp Life of a Confederate Boy, Bratton's Brigade, Longstreet's Corps, C.S.A.* (Gaithersburg, MD: Butternut Press, 1984).

Longacre, Edward G., *A Soldier to the Last: Maj. Gen. Joseph Wheeler in Blue and Gray* (Washington, DC: Potomac Books, Inc., 2007).

Longstreet, James, *From Manassas to Appomattox: Memoirs of the Civil War in America* (Bloomington, IN: Indiana University Press, 1960 reprint of 1896 edition).

Lord, Francis A., *Civil War Collector's Encyclopedia* (New York, NY: Castle Books, 1965).

McClain, Wyatt R., 'Report of Captain Wyatt R. McClain, Fifty-first Georgia Infantry Volunteers, C.S. Army on the engagement at Campbell's Station, November 16, 1863', *Supplement to the Official Records of the Union and Confederate Armies*, Serial Number 6 (Wilmington, NC: Broadfoot Publishing Company, 1996).

MacCutcheon, Byron, *The Story of the Twentieth Michigan Infantry, July 15th, 1862 to May 30th, 1865* (Lansing, MI: Robert Smith Printing Company, 1904).

McLaws, Lafayette, *A Soldier's General: The Civil War Letters of Major General Lafayette McLaws* (Chapel Hill, NC: The University of North Carolina Press, 2002).

Maltman, John, Bently Historical Museum, http/www.17thmicoe.org/letter.htm, p. 4.

Marvel, William, *Burnside* (Chapel Hill, NC: The University of North Carolina Press, 1991).

Mendoza, Alexander, *Confederate Struggle For Command: General James Longstreet and the First Corps in the West* (College Station, TX: Texas A&M University Press, 2008).

Miller, John H., *My War Experiences* (Gardner, MA: Meads Print Co., Gardner, 1912).

Minnich, J.W. 'How Some History Is Written', *Confederate Veteran Magazine*, Volume XIII, Number 3 March 1905 (Wilmington, NC: Broadfoot Publishing Company, 1988).

Minnich, J.W., 'The Cavalry At Knoxville', *Confederate Veteran Magazine* 13.1, January 1924 Wilmington, NC: Broadfoot Publishing Company, 1988.

Minnich, J.W., 'Famous Rifles', *Confederate Veteran Magazine* 30.7, July 1922 (Wilmington, NC: Broadfoot Publishing Company, 1988).

Moore, Frank (ed.), *The Rebellion Record: A Diary of American Events,* 12 Volumes (New York, NY: Arno Press, 1977 reprint).

Morrow, John A., *The Confederate Whitworth Sharpshooters* (2nd Edition; Atlanta, GA: Published by the author, 2002).

Nason, W.A., 'With the Ninth Army Corps in East Tennessee', *Military Order of the Loyal Legion of the United States* (Wilmington, NC: Broadfoot Publishing Company, 1993).

*The New York Herald,* December 6, 1863, 28.338.

Oeffinger, John C. (ed.), *A Soldier's General: The Civil War Letters of Major General Lafayette McLaws* (Chapel Hill, NC: The University of North Carolina Press, 2002).

Osborne, William H., *The History of the Twenty-ninth Regiment of Massachusetts Volunteer Infantry in the Late War of the Rebellion* (Boston, MA: Albert J. Wright, Printer, 1877).

Parker, Ezra K., 'Campaign of Battery D, First Rhode Island Light Artillery, in Kentucky and East Tennessee', *Military Order of the Loyal Legion of the United States*, Volume 41 (Wilmington, NC: Broadfoot Publishing Company, 1993).

Parker, Thomas H., *History of the Fifty-First Regiment of Pennsylvania Volunteers* (Philadephia, PA: King and Baird Printers, 1869).

Pettit, Frederick, *Infantryman Pettit: The Civil War Letters of Corporal Frederick Pettit* (Shippensburg, PA: White Mane Publishing Company, 1990).

Phillips, Stanley, *Civil War Corps Badges and Other Related Awards, Badges, Medals of the Period* (Lanham, MD: Published by the author, 1982).

Poe, Orlando, 'The Defense of Knoxville', in Robert U. Johnson and Clarence C Buel, *Battles and Leaders of the Civil War*, Volume III (New York, NY: The Century Company, 1888).

Poe, Orlando M., *Personal Recollections of the Occupation of East Tennessee and the Defense of Knoxville* (Knoxville, TN: The East Tennessee Historical Society, 1963 reprint of the 1889 edition).

Polley, J.B., *Hood's Texas Brigade: Its Marches, Its Battles, Its Achievements* (Lexington, KY: Forgotten Books, 2012 Reprint of the 1910 edition).

Poole, John R., *Cracker Cavaliers: The 2$^{nd}$ Georgia Cavalry Under Wheeler and Forrest* (Macon, GA: Mercer University Press, 2000).

Reeves, Charles A., Jr. (ed.), *The Battle of Campbell Station* (Knoxville, TN: Charles A. Reeves, Jr., 1986).

Ripley, Warren, *Artillery and Ammunition of the Civil War* (New York, NY: Promontory Press, 1970).

Robertson, John (compiler), *Michigan in the War* (Revised Edition; Lansing, MI: W.S. George & Company, 1882).

Roemer, Jacob, *Reminiscences of the War of the Rebellion, 1861-1865* (Flushing, NY: Estate of Jacob Roemer, 1897).

Report of Jacob Roemer, New York State Military Museum and Veterans Research Center, http://dmna.ny.gov/historic/reghist /civil/artillery/34thIndBat/34thInd; Civil War Medal of Honor Recipients, http://www.history.army.mil/html/moh/civwarmz. html

Rothrock, Mary U. (ed.), *The French Broad-Holston County: A History of Knox County, Tennessee* (Knoxville, TN: East Tennessee Historical Society, 1946).

Sauers, Richard A. (ed.), *The Civil War Journal of Colonel Bolton 51$^{st}$ Pennsylvania, April 20, 1861-August 2, 1865* (Conshohocken, PA: Combined Publishing, 2000).

Scott, H.L., *Military Dictionary: Comprising Technical Definitions; On Raising and Keeping Troops; Actual Service, Including Makeshifts and Improved Materiel; and Law, Government, Regulation, and Administration Relating to Land Forces* (New York, NY: D. Van Nostrand, 1864).

Seiger, Robert S., *South Carolina's Military Organizations During the War Between the States*, 4 Volumes (Charleston, SC: The History Press, 2008).

Seymour, Digby G., *Divided Loyalties: Fort Sanders and the Civil War in East Tennessee* (rev. ed.; Knoxville, TN: East Tennessee Historical Society, 1982).

Shell, Malcolm L., *From Frontier Fort to Town Hall: A Brief history of Farragut, Tennessee 1787-2005* (Farragut, TN: Farragut Folklife Museum, 2005).

Shepard, Irwin, 'Letters from Sergeant Irwin Shepard, Co. E, 17th Michigan Infantry', Typescript of the original letters (University of Michigan, Ann Arbor, Michigan, in the files of the Farragut Folklife Museum).

Sherwood, Isaac R., *Memories of the War* (Toledo, OH: The H.J. Chittenden Co., 1923).

Sifakis, Stewart, *Compendium of the Confederate Armies: Florida and Arkansas* (New York, NY: Facts On File, 1992).

Sifakis, Stewart, *Compendium of the Confederate Armies: Virginia* (New York, NY: Facts On File, 1992).

Sifakis, Stewart, *Compendium of the Confederate Armies: Louisiana* (New York, NY: Facts On File, 1995).

Sifakis, Stewart, *Compendium of the Confederate Armies: South Carolina and Georgia* (New York, NY: Facts On File, 1995).

Simpson, Harold B., *Hood's Texas Brigade: Lee's Grenadier Guard* (Fort Worth, TX: Landmark Publishing, Inc., 1999).

Sorrel, G. Moxley, *Recollections of a Confederate Staff Officer* (Jackson, TN: McCowart-Mercer, Inc., 1958 reprint of the 1905 edition).

Stone, James M., *Personal Recollections of the Civil War: By One Who Took Part in it as a Private Soldier in the 21st Volunteer Regiment of Infantry From Massassachsetts* (Boston, MA: Published by Author, 1918).

Sumner, George C., *Battery D, First Rhode Island Artillery in the Civil War, 1861-1865* (Providence, RI: Rhode Island Printing Company, 1897).

Swisher, James K., *Prince of Edisto: Brigadier General Micah Jenkins C.S.A.* (Berryville, VA: Rockbridge Publishing Company, 1996).

Thomas, Dean S., *Round Ball to Rimfire: A History of Civil War Small Arms Ammunition* (Gettysburg, PA: Thomas Publications, 2010).

Thompson, Bradford F., *History of the 112th Regiment of Illinois Volunteer Infantry in the Great War of the Rebellion 1862-1865* (Toulon, IL: The Stark County News Office, 1885).

Todd, Frederick P., *American Military Equipage 1851-1872*, Volume I (Providence, RI: The Company of Military Historians, 1974).

Todd, William, *The Seventy-Ninth Highlanders New York Volunteers In The War Of The Rebellion* (Albany, NY: Press of Brandow, Barton and Company, 1886).

Travis, Benjamin F., *The Story of the Twenty-Fifth Michigan* (Kalamazoo, MI: Kalamazoo Publishing Company, 1897).

United States War Department: *The War of the Rebellion: A Compilation of the Official Records of the Union and Confederate Armies* 128 Volumes, Volume 31, Part 1 (Harrisburg, PA: The National Historical Society, 1971 reprint of 1880-1901 edition).

Van West, Carroll, *The Tennessee Encyclopedia of History and Culture* (Nashville, TN: The Tennessee Historical Society, 1998).

Walcott, Charles Folsom, *History of the Twenty-first Regiment Massachusetts Volunteers in the War for Preservation of the Union, 1861-1865* (Boston, MA: Houghton, Miffin and Company, 1882).

Warner, Ezar J., *Generals in Blue: Lives of the Union Commanders* (Baton Rouge, LA: Louisiana State University Press, 1988).

Warner, Ezar J., *Generals in Gray: Lives of the Confederate Commanders* (Baton Rouge, LA: Louisiana State University Press, 1988).

Welcher, Frank J., *The Union Army 1861-1865: Organization and Operations, Volume II: The Western Theater* (Bloomington, IN: Indiana University Press, 1993).

Wells, Samuel, *Autobiography of Samuel Wells* (New Carlisle, IN: Gazette Printing Company, 1897).

Welsh, Jack D., *Medical Histories of Confederate Generals* (Kent, OH: The Kent State University Press, 1995).

Welsh, Jack D., *Medical Histories of Union Generals* (Kent OH: The Kent State University Press, 1996).

West, John C., *A Texan in Search of a Fight, Being the Diary and Letters of a Private Soldier in Hood's Texas Brigade* (Baltimore, MD: Butternut and Blue, 1994).

White, Julius., 'Burnside Occupation of East Tennessee', in *Military Essays and Recollections: Papers Military Order of the Loyal Legion of the United States* (Wilmington, NC: Broadfoot Publishing Company, 1992).

Wilson, James H., *Under the Old Flag: Recollections of Military Operations in the War for the Union, The Spanish War, The Boxer Rebellion, Etc.* (Lexington, KY: Forgotten Books, 2012).

Woodward, Philip Grenville, 'The Siege of Knoxville', in *Military Order of the Loyal Legion of the United States*, Volume 30 (Wilmington, NC: Broadfoot Publishing Company, 1992).

Wyckoff, Mac., *A History of the 3rd South Carolina Regiment: Lee's Reliables* (Wilmington, NC: Broadfoot Publishing Company, 2008).

# INDEX

www.ingramcontent.com/pod-product-compliance
Lightning Source LLC
LaVergne TN
LVHW051840080426

835512LV00018B/2982